0032481

E DUE

SHIMINT 99

MEXICAN
INTERIORS

Garden of House in Cuernavaca

MEXICAN

INTERIORS

by Verna Cook Shipway and Warren Shipway

ARCHITECTURAL BOOK PUBLISHING CO., INC.

STAMFORD, CONNECTICUT 06903

Preceding page:

When Señor Don Moises Saenz reconstructed an old house in Taxco, he was given, as a house-warming present, a lock with a decorative wrought-iron escutcheon which carried the inscription in Spanish, "Here the door is a heart always open." It had been made by a student in the School of Direct Sculpting, Mexico, D.F., a school which Señor Saenz as Sub-Secretary of Education was instrumental in organizing.

Accompanying the lock was the ingeniously wrought key shown on the Title Sheet. The bow terminates in a heart, carrying out the motif of the escutcheon, while within the bow, an open book is inscribed on one side with the name of the artisan and on the reverse, with the name of the recipient. Instead of an ordinary bit, here the initials *M S* of Señor Saenz were used.

NINTH PRINTING, 1988

ISBN: 8038-0159-9

Library of Congress Catalog Card Number: 62-16187

Printed in the United States of America

CONTENTS

Contents

"Where did you find these things?" It was a question asked us again and again, both by visitors to Mexico as well as by the Mexicans themselves. Our previous book, *THE MEXICAN HOUSE Old and New*, had lately preceded us into the land of its family tree and it was over these pages they were mulling. It was an unexpected form of greeting as we zigzagged our way south from the Arizona border, photographing and sketching the material presented in the pages which follow.

This often repeated question, "Where did you find these things?," at first surprised us. Surely the houses, their details, the gardens with their incidentals were all about, asking for attention. Only a minor portion was screened from the outside by house or garden walls, a custom set by Moorish precedent. Puzzling over this curious circumstance, we looked in retrospect at our first trip, made about fifteen years ago, into this vital and colorful country, in order to resolve our own first impressions. Of course, we had been moved by some of the massive public buildings with their provocative murals; the gorgeous churches, many with bafflingly intricate and lavish ornamentation smothered in gold-leaf forming backgrounds for bejeweled and bedecked saintly images. All of this we had seen through a veil of foreign vowels, the pat-pat of tortilla making, the cries of street vendors and the muffled clinking of burros' hoofs. It was not until several years and several trips later that we emerged from this trance to accustom our eyes to the charm and the not-by-rule conceptions of the Mexican home and its setting.

VII

More baffling, however, was this question when asked by the residents. Anyone's habitat, we concluded, is apt to become so dulled by everyday acquaintance that its merits are lost in a blurred nonentity. Obviously it was a delight and a wonder for them to see through another's eyes unsuspected treasures standing next door or passed unobserved on the way to market.

Because of these reasons, we thought it might be of interest to gather material for a sort of companion piece, a book rounding out the various influences seeping in from overseas, east and west, then taking root in a latent artistry many centuries old — the strong strain from old Spain both in custom and in unconscious adaptation, the unadulterated pre-Conquest designs still used as motifs, the uninhibited vigor which found an affinity in the impulsive Baroque, the indelible impress of Indian heritage. Furniture, ceramics, lighting fixtures, silver, fabrics and many other ingredients contribute their distinctive flavors to this bounteous potpourri.

Many of the subjects comprising this book were on display in regional museums and others in galleries and shops. The cooperation given us was most warming. A great part of the material was found in private homes. We hope that the owners will be pleased with our selections from the wealth of fascinating items and views available. For their gracious consent in permitting us to secure an indication of the background of their private lives, we offer our deep gratitude.

Below, Spanish names of owners are listed alphabetically by surname or father's name. Where a following, additional surname is used, it is the family name of the owner's mother.

X

This is a book about houses. It contains decorative motifs and livable elements from homes in Mexico, things that adapt themselves well to tasteful surroundings in many parts of the world. The miniature Colima house, pictured here, was made some seven hundred years ago. Notice the zigzag design painted on the roof, the incised fret on the roof overhang and walls.

Even in centuries past, it seems, people wanted something different, some unusual touches to express their individual tastes.

Before old, heavy-paneled entrance doors of a former hacienda, stands this 17th-century Michoacán Madonna, carved from a single piece of wood. Despite its antiquity, the original polychroming is clearly discernible — the delicate flesh tints of the placid face, the mauve of the robe under a cloak of dark blue.

1

Home of Agustín Cullen

SALAS, CORREDORES
and FIREPLACES

Home of Manuel Subervielle y de Mier

Many small towns in Mexico are blessed with more or less constant climates the year around. There covered porches, or *corredores,* open but sheltered from the summer rains, are spacious and alluring centers of daily living. Overlooking patios or gardens enclosed by masonry walls, removed from traffic noises of the nearby streets, they convey a feeling of seclusion and quiet which makes for the ultimate in relaxation. The *corredores* shown on these pages are favored examples. Interesting and unusual details divert the eye without intruding on the prevailing calm.

A small, recessed fireplace at the open end of a *corredor* has its top-shaped masonry hood decorated with old spurs. Bands of cocoa brown against the soft peach of the walls repeat the ceiling colors.

Another wing of the *corredor* on the facing page. Handsome Talavera de Puebla jardinières are filled with full-blown paper flowers, distinctly Mexican, in pinks, whites, and soft yellows. At random, within this mass of bloom, perch tender little doves of white paper.

Home of William Burgess

Against a chartreuse wall, an old and exquisitely carved wood cabinet (now used to house the hi-fi equipment) is flanked by recessed openings with shell-shaped heads, painted a blackish olive-green. Large earthenware jars filled with white gladiolas contrast with the intense black of the flagstone floor.

A late 16th-century statue of Santiago is at last safe atop the cabinet. During the years when he occupied an honored position on the coffee table, the curious had almost pulled out the tail of his charger.

Villa Montaña

Overlooking the city of Morelia, in a high ceilinged *sala* with richly textured stone walls, the more somber tones of the unframed Guadalupe above the fireplace and the green robe of the *Santo*, are a foil for the red of the clay screen.

Casa Trini

Home of Giorgio Belloli

The carved wood of this chest, vandalized from the altar of an old church, was found nailed upside down to patch a floor. Restored by the resourceful owner, it now forms the drawer fronts of this rich piece of mesquite furniture under a luxurious, carved wood mirror frame with its baroque shell cresting.

(*Right*) One of a pair of old, woolly stone spaniels, a trusty guardian of any entry.

The three-tiered composition of this corner fireplace is singular.
Two very serious little musicians, figures from the belfry of a
17th-century Indian chapel, support the pink stone lintel.

Home of Francisco García Valencia

One of the delightful fancies in the reconstruction of this home is a tree, quaintly modeled in plaster by the mason *maestro* without preconceived sketch, on an end wall of the raised dining area. Flower-like brackets here and there support the owner's collection of small, wood-carved saints, producing a charming effect.

House of Giorgio Belloli

This enchanting caracole of cantilevered stone treads around a circular chimney was the unique solution of Señor Belloli's problem. He had to provide access to second floor bedrooms but refused to sacrifice the fascination of a fireplace, despite his limited area.

Home of Giorgio Belloli

Paramount in their Marfil home is the impeccable taste of the owners. Using the partially fallen walls of an old ore-reduction hacienda, the construction is on the grand scale. These views of the *sala* do not include the large, circular-headed glazed opening which makes the splendid patio and its fountain a part of this room.

Rising from waxed, greenish-gray floor flags, high Spanish-white walls support an arched ceiling of salmon-pink brick. The imposing chimney breast opposite with a balustraded extension, separate living and dining areas. The focal point of the stone mantle is a keyblock from a ruined church, on which the keys of Saint Peter, surmounted by the three-tiered Papal tiara, are carved in bold relief.

Home of Giorgio Belloli

The furniture, mostly of polished mesquite, was not only designed by the owner but crafted in his workshop. The mellow tones of the richly stained cowhide seats of the metal-frame chairs and upholstered bench blend with the subtle colors of the pre-Conquest and Colonial figures and with a lampshade made of palm fibers from a burro pad.

A further enrichment is this small Saint Christopher, with pants rolled high, as he carries the Christ Child across a river. The rich vermilion robe of the Child against the gold costume of the saint, in *estofada,* is magnificent.

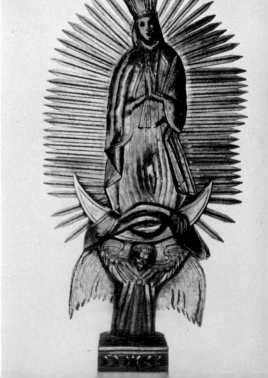

El Arte Tonalteca

Under the high ceiling of the *sala* in the Casa de Villanueva (now known as the Casa Humboldt, because it provided a brief lodging for the renowned Alexander Von Humboldt in 1803), the fireplace breast depicts a portion of the universe; a benign sun, with stars above and the moon and earth below, gives us our life as shown by a flower, a fish, and a bird. Old in conception but new in execution.

(*Right*) A small statue in wood, the Virgin of Guadalupe, patroness of the Americas, stands in an attitude of adoration against her radiant background on a new moon supported by an angel.

Home of Hector Alcocer

Home of Francisco García Valencia

The simplicity of the bedroom above, with its corner fireplace, is highlighted by a Chet Thompson painting of his young son. The boy's yellow flowers and red jacket, all against a background of green-yellow and silver-gray tones, give the key to the room's furnishings.

(*Right*) A recessed fireplace in the former home of the Conde de Rul. Unusual because of its deep shell head and the raised hearth's blue-and-white tile facing.

Home of Marcel de la Harpe

Another assembly of richly weathered stone fragments of the past. A keystone was inserted and shaped to widen the fire opening, guarded by two solemn caryatids.

(*Left*) Among potted plants in a sheltered patio, stands this serene image of San José, delicately modeled. During the anti-clerical period of the past century, the silver leaf and gold leaf of the statue's garments were painted black to hide their brilliance. Only recently its owner, Louise Belloli, painstakingly removed this paint, restoring its former splendor.

Home of Joaquín Cortina Garíbar

Quaint, informal fireplaces carry, during the summer months, the refreshing key colors of their bedrooms. Above, fluffy paper flowers in lavenders, pinks, and lilac tones are enlivened by a note of red. At left, a similar bouquet runs a gamut of pinks to light reds.

SALAS, CORREDORES AND FIREPLACES 17

Home of Agustín Cullen

The play of light on the walls of the *sala*, shown here and on the opposite page, gives them a chameleon-like quality. At times they become vibrant with various tones of pink, ranging from salmon to the near tangerine color of the sofa's slip cover.

A carved wood niche and panel, richly gilded, adds sparkle to these sensitive color tones.

Against the pinks of an inner wall, a white plaster mantle stands out in bold relief above the brick tile of floor and hearth, waxed to a deep tobacco brown. The fireplace facing of blue tile with stylized white and blue inserts, is emphasized by a shaped, white plaster border under three novel brackets.

Photograph by Graficas Comerciales　　　　　　　　　*Home of Frederick de la Rozière*

Restraint and choice discrimination belong to this minor room of blue-gray walls and carpeting, with niches of wine red.

Batik, a rare and difficult textile art medium, has of late, become increasingly popular in Mexico. In great part this is due to the work of Vaki, creator of this panel with cows in shocking pink against burgundy.

"El Opalo"

The Oriental trend, first felt in Mexico during the 16th century because of the shipments of precious products from Manila to Acapulco on their way to Spain, continues its subtle influence. Of striking contrast to the deep tones of the masonry walls, the black stone floor and the greenish-gold grass cloth, is the expanse of white in the ceiling and furnishings.

Home of Balbina Madero de Azcarraga

Photograph by Guillermo Zamora

Home of Arturo Pani

Graceful cast brass vases holding oval-shaped candle shields of grapes and wheat, customarily used as altar pieces, serve also as fireplace fittings.

A tall-ceilinged bedroom with calm simplicity, all very high in key. Brick tile floor, stained dark, with occasional rugs matching the butter yellow of the walls. The fabric of the chairs carries an overall design of animals and flowers in white on a refreshing blue background. The wood of the furniture, including the carved angel holding a plate glass top under an etched glass lamp base, shows through a thin rubbed glaze.

A wandering Victorian strain is set to style in San Miguel de Allende.

Home of Joaquín Cortina Garíbar

Two delightfully intimate glimpses of a main *sala*.

Home of Thomas Briscoe Miller

Robustly carved newels, found in a warehouse, are examples of the exuberance
of the Baroque. Colorful ceramic jars were made for the owner in Puebla.

House in Cuernavaca

Villa Montaña

A brick beehive forms a diverting contrast to the
background of chinked stone, all whitewashed.
(*Left*) An enchanting pierced stone ventilating
panel, twenty-four inches wide.

Home of Juan Hübbe López

The thick masonry walls of Colonial Mexican homes make possible the use of traditional *conchas*, roughly the shape of the concave side of a shell, as a heading for openings and recessed wall niches. Here, at the end of an open entrance corridor, a wide-spread *concha* in cast plaster over a pair of heavy, paneled doors, frames a view of the garden beyond.

Home of Hector Alcocer

This radiant *concha*, the work of native craftsmen, in the 18th-century former
home of the Conde de Rul, is in the same room as that on the following page.
Additional views of these doors are shown on page 81.

section

0   1   2   3   4 ft

30

A detailed view of a shell-crested window, and one of
the exquisitely carved shutters at this opening.

House of Giorgio Belloli

A mothlike effect with simple white cotton wings hanging from swinging arms below a massive *concha*.

Both modeled by hand in plaster, the *concha* opposite is of earlier date, while that below was done during the recent reconstruction of an old hacienda.

Museo Casa Chata

La Hacienda de San Gabriel

During the period of the Crusades, a pilgrim to the Holy Land identified himself by the small shell which he carried. Later used as a decorative motif, shells were given an endless variety of forms. They vary widely from the undirected and highly imaginative work of the Mexican artisans to more restrained, classic molds.

Museo Casa Chata

Museo Regional de Guadalajara

33

Interesting ceilings, the grace of *conchas*, impressive doors, and an occasional fireplace are the salient architectural features of a typical room of Colonial traditions. Here are shown types of the more customary ceiling constructions. Brick, about eight inches by twenty inches, spans heavy beams.

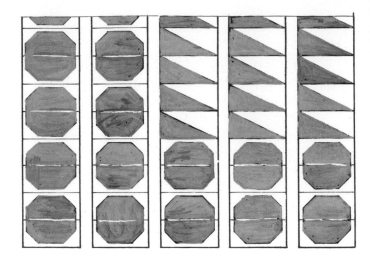

Above is shown the ceiling of a small covered porch. Although apparently in two colors, only the white areas are painted. With the natural red of the brick, they form a central panel of triangles bordered by two courses of octagonal shapes.

In the examples above and below, the patterns are again formed by painting in white certain portions of the brick. In both cases, the hand-hewn wooden beams are stained to a blackish brown.

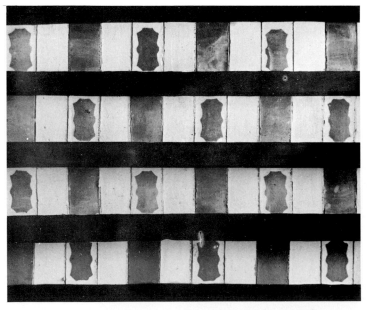

Home of Salvador Miranda

Home of Joaquín Cortina Garíbar

Above, in order to escape the ubiquitous termite, concrete beams were used instead of wood. The toothed design of the ceiling brick, left unpainted, contrasts sharply with a field of soft apricot color, repeating that of the walls. Beams, painted dark green, have soffits decorated in yellow and sky blue.

Home of Humberto Arellano Garza

A unique ceiling of precast plaster tile in low relief: The raised center cross in deep cocoa on a white field with an inner frame of grayish-mauve, picking up the tone of the over-door shells; all with a deeper surround repeating the color of the cross.

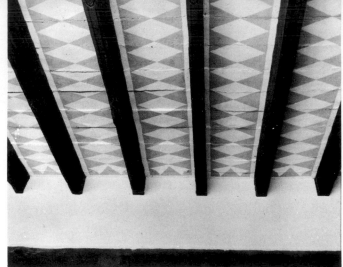

Home of William Burgess

With a height of nine and a half feet at the exterior wall of the dining area, this ceiling soars up at a uniform pitch over an intermediate girder to sixteen feet on the far opposite wall of the *sala*. The resulting effect is one of intimacy in the former space coupled with great scale and dignity in the latter.

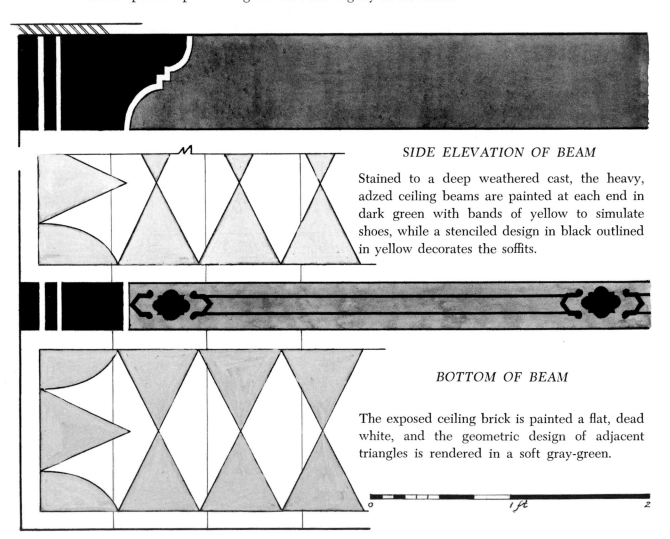

SIDE ELEVATION OF BEAM

Stained to a deep weathered cast, the heavy, adzed ceiling beams are painted at each end in dark green with bands of yellow to simulate shoes, while a stenciled design in black outlined in yellow decorates the soffits.

BOTTOM OF BEAM

The exposed ceiling brick is painted a flat, dead white, and the geometric design of adjacent triangles is rendered in a soft gray-green.

Home of Salvador Miranda

During the reconstruction of a portion of El Convento del Carmen, this ornate ceiling was installed over a dining room. The precast plaster panels and small bosses were copied from some found in the old Convento de Santo Domingo in Oaxaca.

Here, the walls and ceiling are painted a shell-white, while light terra cotta accents feature the ornamentation. Added elegance is contributed by the beautifully embossed and incised silver chandelier with its pierced galleries, brackets, and delicately wrought chains.

Casa de los Tesoros

Above whitewashed walls, peeled saplings, water-stained and weathered, carry closely laid twigs on the diagonal. This roof construction is common to the area. First, an overlay of native grasses, then eight inches of earth for insulation, and finally a course of flat brick protected by a trowel coat of lime and cement, known as *mescla*.

During the later years of the 18th and early 19th centuries, this *portal* or arcade was typical of many others in Alamos, Sonora. Originally forming the front of the home of a beloved padre, Juan Nicolas Quiros y Mora, the tweedlike ceiling now serves as an introduction to a hotel famed for its cuisine.

Hacienda del Chorrillo

Due to the size of the *sala* in this charming *posada*, heavy ceiling construction was necessary. The impressive girders are decorated with a stenciled design in rusts and yellows, inspired by the plumes of the feathered serpent's tail carved on the facing stone of the ancient pyramid at Xochicalco, Morelos, a panel of which is shown opposite.

A dining room of great refinement. Giving on the garden *corredor*, it is dominated by a magnificent Baccarat chandelier in blue glass with exquisitely cut crystal drops and globes. The graceful Pompeian-red niche, with its shell head, is set in a wall of soft peach.

Home of Joaquín Cortina Garibar

Casa Trini

Fanciful creation of artists, Elsa Wachter and Thea Ramsey. A composition of white wax-and-fabric flowers, interspersed with pearls and green leaves, rises from a gilded wood urn under a glass dome.

With a wide arch framing one end, the dining room opens on a conservatory where a stone fountain is surrounded by tropical greenery. The chalk white of the walls and ceiling is a foil for a harmonious medley of pink tones — the walls of the planting area, the pink stone of the arch, the mass of pink gladiolas forming the table decoration, the chair cushions, and then, increasing in depth, to the darker pink of the rug on heavily waxed floor brick.

The chair above is a reproduction of an old one owned by the designer, Rodolfo Ayala.

Home of Juan Hübbe López

Home of Judith Van Beuren

Rugged simplicity with elegance.

The refectory table and buffet shelf on this and the opposite page are formed with heavy, hand-hewn planks, stained to a wiped-off black. The several planks of the table top, 32 inches in width and 120 inches long, are bolted to two horizontal members 17 inches in from each end which are both supported by a vertical post embedded in the floor. This arrangement enables ten persons to be seated with no structural interference. Hung from the ceiling on heavy chain, a horizontal pole carries five lamps encased in cylindrical bamboo shades which give interlocking circles of light along the full length of the table.

The delicate black borders and the heavy black monograms, *JVB*, of the owner, are in striking contrast to the warm white of this glazed ceramic tableware. Overhead, colorful 1879 paintings of fruit arrangements give richness and depth to the chalk-white walls.

The charm of this small dining room is enhanced by the grace of the shell head and scroll outline crowning the niche, all in white against soft gray walls, accented by richly colored Mexican majolica.

Home of Francisco García Valencia

Up two risers from the *sala* level, the white-walled dining area is lighted by glass brick distributed throughout the flat ceiling. The color note is set by the brass-gold and charcoal-black of the conventionalized oil painting by the owner, showing three shrouded figures. The plaster tree and *santos* on page 10 decorate the left end wall of this area.

(*Left*) The three small pieces of carved stone which were bought at a demolition sale for ten *pesos* or eighty cents now adorn the curved head of this simple opening.

Villa Montaña

Color, texture, and care woven into a jaunty table staging. A transom of mellowed wood is set off by a rough brick wall; the jig-sawed half-circle becomes a backdrop for massed pineapples, papayas, mangoes, and melons. On the forestage are lovely old Dutch candlesticks, a crimped copper bowl of red geraniums, and amber goblets on a planked table top.

Carápan

The unrestricted and interlacing wanderings of a philodendron vine give charm and tranquillity to outdoor
living and dining on this ample *corredor*.

This beguiling flower pot container is an example of
the current contribution to the artifacts of Mexico from
Monterrey.

Fringed henequen mats in deep coral compliment the *Loza de Barro* or fine earthenware made in the workshop of Maja Gruebler.

Where the garden is an extra room, as in most of Mexico, terrace dining is joyous. This informal setting is regional — chairs, serving plates and goblets from Guadalajara and its environs.

A studio home of an accomplished sculptress in the hills of Taxco has a small kitchen of great charm. Rough gray stone walls above dark red masonry bases of both sink and *brasero* are enlivened by lustrous glazed pottery. Little toy jugs and plates decorate the cement wings of the open cupboard in which thin flagstone shelves carry colorful examples of native ceramics.

Home of Humberto Arellano Garza

Bona S.A.

In this large kitchen, the *brasero* or masonry cooking top, with its charcoal grill and gas plates, is a central island under a ventilating hood of ample proportions. In contrast with the beige tile background and colorful tile inserts designed by the well known artist, Olga Costa, is the gleam of copper pots in the open cupboards, known as *alacenas*.

(*Right*) A whimsical white wire chicken with red comb and tin eye here replaces the customary Mexican egg basket.

This ornate ceramic pitcher with the figure of Father Hidalgo, commemorates the centenary of the Revolution of 1810. A similar pitcher is in the center of the top shelf below.

Home of Judith Van Beuren

Above, an *alacena* in the kitchen of the Museo de la Ceramica, with mugs and plates of *petatillo* ware on the middle shelves, under a shelf of glass spice jars surrounded by various utensils.

One of the several elliptical-headed *alacenas* in the kitchen on the opposite page. The owner's collection of spice jars is choice.

Home of Judith Van Beuren

Designed for hospitality. At one end of the dining room whose table and buffet are shown on pages 44 and 45, this masonry counter has three gas burners resembling a typical *brasero*, and a tiled sink, here filled with philodendron. Under a chalk-white brick hood, on which are hung various copper skillets and ceramics, this wall becomes decorative as well as purposeful.

(*Left*) One of the ornaments on the hood above. A black glazed-pottery lion from Puebla is eager to accumulate and protect the savings of some child.

Home of Judith Van Beuren

A roofless kitchen extension drenched in sunlight, elegantly lighthearted in blues on white.

A gourmet's grouping at the far end of a long plank table. Fruits of the tropics cluster around a Puebla urn.

House in Cuernavaca

Tiled walls in Mexico do not consist of monotonous squares of deadly machine-made likeness; instead each component offsets its neighbor with a subtle play of light and shade by virtue of its handmade surfacing. The effect is handsome.

Manuel Subervielle y de Mier

Now and then captivating motifs are commissioned from Puebla to accent the soft sheen of tiled kitchen walls. A personalized legend may float over a pictured abundance as on the blue ribbon above, held by little gray doves, which literally says, "In the house of Don Manuel, he is she and she is he." Or, the swag may modestly state, "*Sal, pimienta y buen entendimiento hacen buena cocina.*"

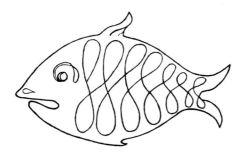

Daylight through ceilings. These cupolas are the direct offspring of the tile-roofed lanterns of many churches. In addition to providing good ventilation and a generous central source of light, they unpretentiously form striking architectural features.

An atmosphere of tranquillity engendered by a gardened terrace with the calm of overall patterning on the tiled cupolas in the foreground, is in soothing contrast to the jumbled roof tops and church spires beyond.

Below, a domed kitchen ceiling topped by a square cupola is covered with tile on both inside and outside. Colorful feature tiles are again used to enhance the plain surfaces.

House in Cuernavaca   *Home of Lorenza L. Story*

Home of Juan Hübbe López

The high glaze of the slightly uneven surfaces of these floor and wall tiles in warm white reflects a rich lustrous quality. Below hydrangea blooms backed by massed planting run glazed borders in pinks and greens, while a large ceramic shell serves as a soap dish.

A detail of an exceptionally handsome bathroom. On a background of light gray Mexican marble, a large brass dolphin looks down upon a gold-colored tub.

House in Cuernavaca

An old panel of tiles which honors S^r, S^n Juan Nepomuseno. On his refusal, under torture and eventual death, to reveal the confessional secrets of a Spanish queen who was suspected of infidelity by her husband, he was adopted by lawyers as their patron saint.

An angel on one side with finger to lips commemorates his silence, while another holds the cross to exemplify his sacrifice. A halo of stars above his head contains the letters A, B, O, G, A, D, O, which spell the Spanish word meaning lawyer.

On a field of white tile, embedded in a wall of pink plaster, appear blues, mauves, browns, and black. The large inset, about forty-two inches wide, creates an indelible impression in the entryway of this superb home.

Despite the humidity in old masonry walls and later blistering, there remain some noble paintings in fresco in early churches and monasteries. In the main patio of this 17th-century convent, a carved wood image of the Archangel Gabriel, in robes of red and gold, stands in a recess of salmon pink. The latter is outlined with frescoed borders and scrolls in reds, black, orange, and deep oyster, against off-white walls.

Partially effaced by water-staining is a painted niche, topped with a simulated shell in orange-red outlined in gray, above bouquets in pinks and reds.

Museo Colonial del Carmen

Museo Historico de Churubusco

On gray-blue walls, frescoed draperies in reds, blues, and yellows hang from a cresting of anthemion motifs to gracefully embrace the painting in its rippling, gilded frame.

La Hacienda de San Gabriel

In a recently restored hacienda, these frescoed borders have been executed with marked sensitivity in the manner of their 16th-century prototypes. Bold geometric running designs are, for the most part, painted in striking black and white.

Up the sides of the bordered door above climbs a frilly vine ending at the top in a cartouche in reds, blues, and pinks.

museo historico de churubusco

museo historico de churubusco

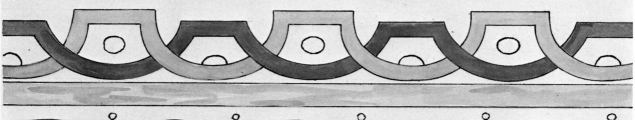

la hacienda de san gabriel

la hacienda de san gabriel

la hacienda de san gabriel

Fresco Borders

Museo Colonial del Carmen

Pink flowers on pale green stems with green leaves fan out in grand scale over off-white walls, above a dado of Pompeian red.

Toward the mid-16th century a differing phase of mural painting was initiated in New Spain. The walls of passages and of refectories began to be decorated by murals painted in fresco in the Renaissance style. Within the monastery of Actopan are outstanding examples.

Above, off-white acanthus scrolls upon a ground of deep mulberry form a frieze around the upper corredor. At the left, a portion of the lofty stair walls, which terminate in a groined vault. In black and white with faint touches of earth-reds, browns and blues, this overall patterning is truly magnificent.

TILES AND FRESCOES   65

Home of Salvador Miranda

Employed so extensively by the Moors in Spain as a means of partial concealment, lattice work has wide adaptations in today's Mexico. In the early churches it was used in choir lofts; the voices could be heard while the singers remained invisible. In convents, it made it possible for the nuns to attend mass. They could see the priest and join in the service but they, themselves, could not be seen by the general participants. The lattice above screens the side of an old confessional booth.

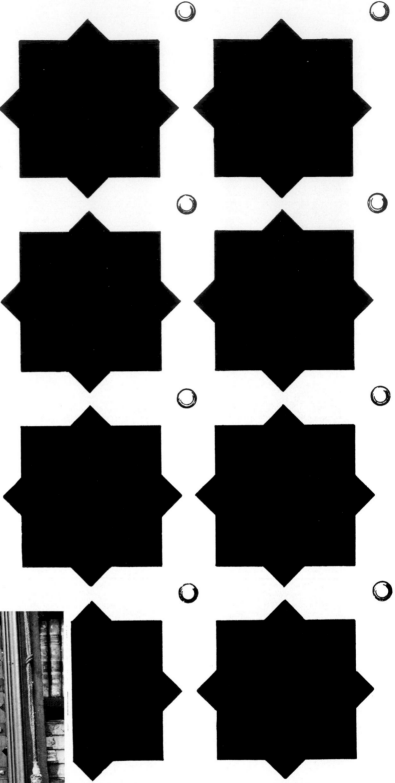

At left and as detailed above, a more open version, embellished with brass studs at each intersection, protects the books behind.

A different look is attained by the relationship of voids to the flush surfaces of the crossed members. For partial screening at a driveway entrance, a pair of gates may have a large scale overall arrangement of star shaped openings six inches wide, in contrast to the one and a half inch squares of the two designs drawn above.

Home of Robert F. Whitehouse

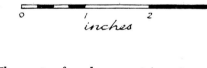

The roots of such geometric patterning have spread to other craft mediums. This clay flower pot container has, no doubt, a Moorish ancestor.

67

The hinged panels in the former home of the beloved Bishop of Quiroga, now a museum in Pátzcuaro, are of recent make but traditional in design. Instead of being formed with band-sawed strips, halved at the joints, the rippling effect of this screening is achieved by jig-sawing thin planks. Their purpose is practical — to see out from the inside, but not in from the outside.

section

0   1   2   3   4   5   6 *in*

scale of drawing

The tracery of this flush wood trellis in Hermosillo is a heritage from the Moors.

Home of Agustín Cullen

In cases and chests of importance as well as closets and service cabinets needing a flow of air, the Moorish-type lattice becomes an integral member, practical and decorative.

Arturo Pani, Designer

Photograph by Guillermo Zamora

Two modern screens, one calm and the other exciting. Above, black lacquered wood frames with gold stripes, have panels of natural-colored bamboo splits interwoven with bands of wool yarn.

At the left, a bizarre group of carved and gilded conceptions fills the panels of a subtle bluish-green wood screen.

The base of the screen on the opposite page is purposefully most deceptive. Although it apparently consists of a series of raised panels between attached balusters, there are actually only flush surfaces. Neither the beribboned and sealed old Spanish documents nor the carelessly attached swags are free-standing — truly a "trompe l'oeil."

Painted on a plywood screen, this romantic view of San Miguel de Allende during the early part of the 19th century, is filled with interest for a familiar of that "most beautiful, loyal, and Christian City." It was completed in 1956 by Robert Davison, at that time a local artist.

In 1797, Miguel Gerónimo Zendejas painted a mural consisting of twelve panels which, in pairs, formed the double doors of six storage cupboards of a store in Puebla. Six of these panels were later used to compose the screen shown on the left, an excellent example of the wall painting of the period.

From Photographic Archives of the Instituto Nacional de Antropologia e Historia

Around the mid-18th century, painted screens representing the colorful daily life of the Mexican scene were the vogue. Here the two principal themes, among others, show work in the farm-yard and the fashionable plea-sures of boating on the canals among the floating gardens of Xochimilco.

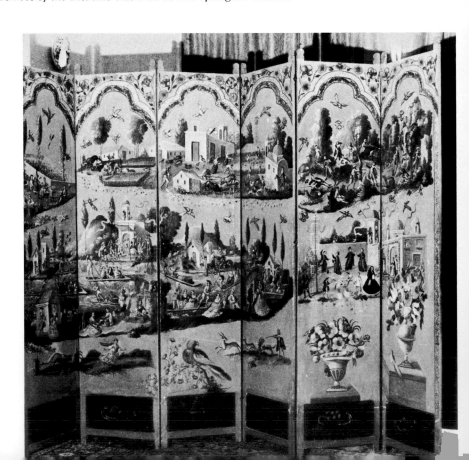

Home of Thomas Briscoe Miller

An upper panel of a rare old door carved from a single and very thin piece of wood. The stylized rosette lies on a field of regimented waves.

Home of Humberto Arellano Garza

These handsomely paneled and massive doors had their origin in Oaxaca over three hundred years ago. The cypress has weathered to a soft silver-gray, showing traces of a former greenish paint in the deeper recesses. Although bronze bosses had utilitarian as well as decorative uses at those times, here they were added later to enhance the design.

A

1 7/8"

A

outside   inside

bronze rosette

*Details
of
Doors pictured
on
Facing and
Following Plates*

Home of Humberto Arellano Garza

The four plaster shells and side splays are painted a grayish-mauve to pick up the overall color of the door. Above the black flintlike flagging of the floor, the interior structual members of the doors on pages 76 and 77, rugged and austere, are most imposing.

Casa Trini

The Dominican seal forms the central motif of the free design (probably influenced by early German settlers) of this former sacristy door from San Cristobal las Casas.

Among the exceptionally fine entrance doors in San Miguel de Allende are the unsymmetrical pair above of the Casa del Pachon, with their baroque scrolls and pendants.

outside   inside

0   3   6   9   1   2   3 ins

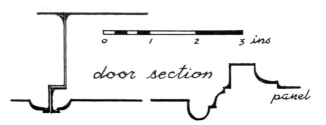

0   1   2   3 ins

door section

panel

Bountiful in interlaced panels, yet calm in overall effect is this double-doored entrance heading a somewhat imposing stairway at the Ex-Convento de los Once Patios, which is now being restored in Pátzcuaro.

Home of Hector Alcocer

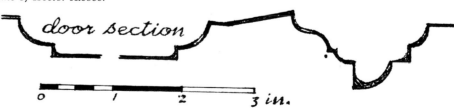

door section

0   1   2   3 in.

The impressive modesty of the pair of doors above show a marked tempering of scale and softening of the carved relief. In contrast, the single leaf on the right, although in the same house (the former home of the Conde de Rul), typifies a bolder and more effusive Baroque. The section is taken through the raised panel on the left.

Home of Agustín Cullen

Originally leaves of a screen, these closet doors in over-all, florid carving in relatively low relief, reflect the joyous Mexican interpretation of old world forms and traditional strains — among the latter, the constantly appearing Moorish mask.

82   DOORS

The substitution of turned spindles for panels between carved wood rails and
stiles of an old door not only provides better circulation of air, but also permits
an alluring vista of the room beyond.

The undulating rails and stiles of this screen door add pleasure to an otherwise functional necessity in a San Miguel de Allende home, remodeled under the exacting care and good taste of Francisco García Valencia. On the far wall of the entrance passage or *zaguan*, painted a Mexican pink, hang colorful plaques of the Three Wisemen.

Home of Lorenza L. Story

Full length shutters, with their separately hung *postigos* or swinging panels, guard this recessed window of the Ex-Convento de los Once Patios, overlooking the tiled roofs of Pátzcuaro. Squares of animal vertebrae, alternating with others of black stone chips, form the flooring immediately under the opening.

An old, heavy door with an open panel of turned wood spindles in the upper portion now hangs in a garden opening of the Museum of Churubusco, formerly a 16th-century convent.

Across from the Basilica in Pátzcuaro, a shop selling religious objects is protected by this charming pair of doors with their incised diamond shapes, timid rosettes, crested with a delicate, applied, symbolic motif.

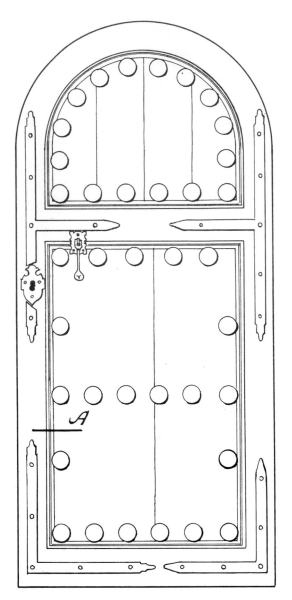

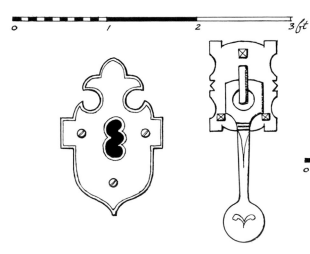

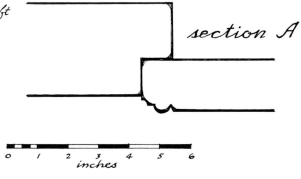

section A

A circular-headed, diminutive door in the Instituto Allende relies upon comparatively oversized nail heads for its distinction.

Along an old twisting street in San Angel stands a pair of carriage doors distinguished by paneling in heroic scale, under a bracketed lantern of even more surprising size. Iron straps emphasized by brass rosettes are of later date.

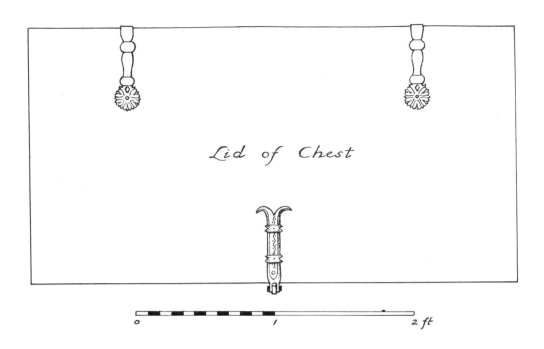

Lid of Chest

Remarkably handsome hardware on a simple pine chest, twenty-three inches high — one of the many choice pieces in the Villa Montaña. The lid straps of the hasp and hinges are shown above, and, on the opposite page, additional drawings of the iron fittings.

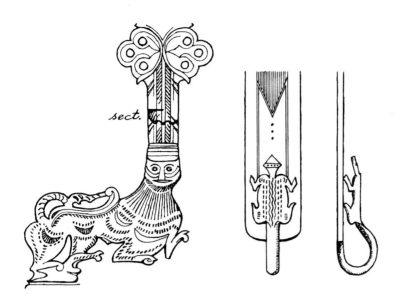

lid and side strap ends

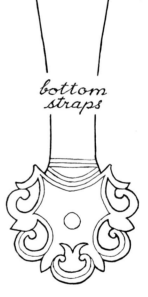

bottom straps

scale of details

On the hasp, an incised Lion of Castile is complacently indifferent to the wrought and applied lizard below. Details of the pierced straps at the sides and bottom are shown above.

Hasp and lockplate on the chest below.

Museo de la Ceramica

An unpainted wood chest of the early 18th century. Although the hardware is not as fine as that on the preceding page, the low stand with baroque apron and turned legs is of interest.

La Casa de Morelos

A small wood chest, eighteen and a half inches wide by twelve inches high, covered with age-blackened cowhide held in place by brass studs and iron mountings, has, on the underside of the lid three amusing, painted figures. In reds, whites and browns on a faded blue background, a lady tightrope walker with her balancing pole is flanked by a clown with his bladder and a stocking-capped dancer.

COLORS
Decoration: Red, green,
blue, blue-green,
sky-blue, beige,
black, and white.
Chest exterior:
Black ground.
Chest interior:
Orange ground.
Stand: Red ground.

SIDE   REAR

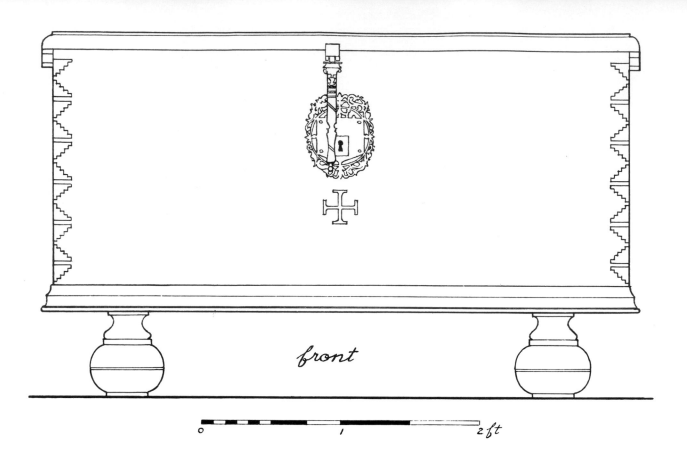

front

A chest of exceptionally careful craftsmanship. The corner jointing of the wide and thick boards, each a single piece, is intricate in design. Branded with a potent cross below the lockplate, while a Latin cross, a symbol and the date 1785, are burned in the lid.

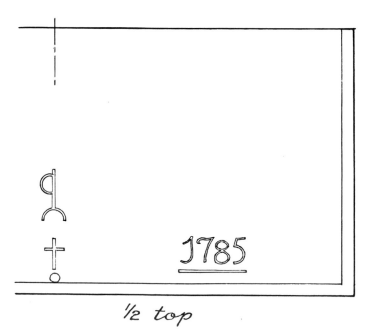

end   _½ top_

The expertly wrought-iron hasp and pierced lockplate give to this chest, detailed here and on the facing page, added distinction.

lid

Museo de la Ceramica

0   1   2   3 *in*

Brought to the west coast of the New World by sea-faring Chinese and Spanish traders, lacquer work was soon adopted by the native artisans. Without the availability of the oriental sumac trees which give off a whitish-gray resin known as *lac,* the Indian craftsman obtained his basic material from a local plant louse, called *aje.*

The chest above is a copy of an 18th-century piece. It was made in Olinalá, Guerrero, where some of the best work in this medium is still done.

Quaintly pretty is this painted chest and stand of the 18th century, from Quiroga, Michoacán. Now faded, soft coloring is accented by red flowers, dark green leaves and birds in brown upon a background of celadon green.

Museo Nacional de Artes e Industrias Populares

Museo Regional de Guadalajara

Beneath the true red of the lid's edge, the floral design is painted in off-whites, rose-reds, yellows, and soft greens on an intense blue background.

Painted during the first third of the 19th century, a decorative border of flowers sweeps around a panel depicting innocent pleasure and high danger. On each side, a gentleman, one with a guitar and the other with a bunch of grapes, escorts his lady through the verdure, paying no attention to the tragedy in the center. There, a rider is being thrown headlong as his barrel-shaped white horse is gored by a fat, gray bull.

Photographic Archives of Instituto Nacional de Antropologia e Historia

Museo Nacional de Artes e Industrias Populares

Quite unusual are the two tiny sea horses
just below the pin of the hasp, while, the
sun and the two-headed Hapsburg eagle
are familiar motifs.

The delicacy with which the Mexicans handle iron is well shown by most of the examples on this and the preceding pages, some old and some of more recent date. The natives of Amozoc near Puebla, of San Luis Potosí, of Guanajuato, and the state of Michoacán have shown a highly developed taste for forged and pierced adornments in iron with which doors and furniture continue to be enriched.

Instituto Allende

*vertical
section*

panel

rail

0   1   2

inches

A serenely satisfying composition of an old
and mellow cabinet, seemingly linked by
tall brass candle holders with an entranc-
ing portrait of a nun, as she takes her vows
to become a bride of the Church.

Home of Giorgio Belloli

Sections of a pair of robust, old entrance doors from Michoacán, now form the sides and front of this ample kitchen cupboard. Gazing down from the top is a carved wood bust of San Gabriel, angel of the Annunciation.

CABINETS AND DESKS   103

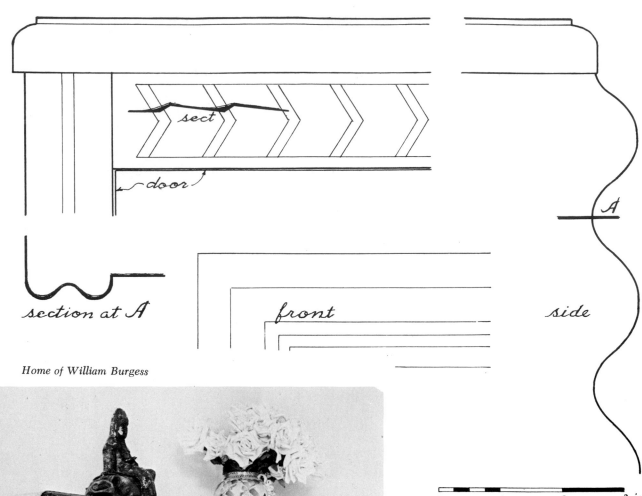

sect

door

section at A

front

side

A

Home of William Burgess

0   1   2   3 in.

panel

section at door panels

Twin rippled contours extend forward in a novel manner to form front supports for this cleverly fashioned cabinet. Also of recent making are the double doors in bold relief. Old panels with large formalized rosettes are used as the ends.

Museo Regional de Guadalajara

Capriciously outlined wall wings and cresting
frame the front and sides of this intriguing design. It may be judged as contradictory with its
angles against curves and its lack of rhythm, too
ponderous to stand on timid cabriole feet. But
greater than these is its glory in being provocative and stimulating.

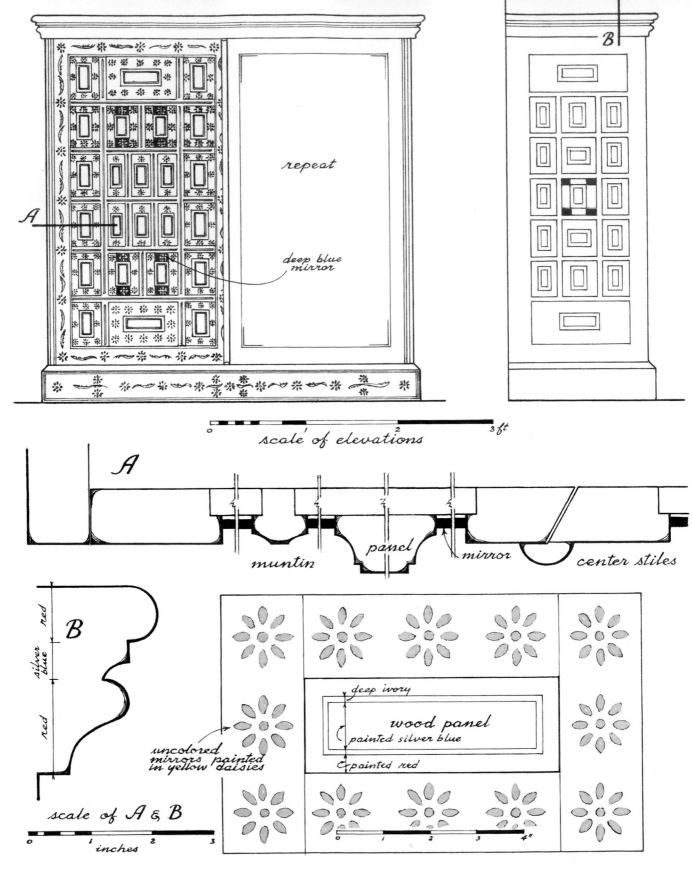

repeat

deep blue
mirror

A

scale of elevations

0   2   3 ft

A

muntin   panel   mirror   center stiles

B

red
silver
blue
red

uncolored
mirrors painted
in yellow daisies

scale of A & B

0   1   2   3
inches

deep ivory

wood panel
painted silver blue

painted red

0   1   2   3   4"

Both sparkling and reticent is this mirrored, airy cabinet splashed with painted, conventionalized daisies, now in the chapel of the former summer home of the Conde de la Canal.

beige

blue

blue

deep ivory

beige

PHOTOGRAPH AND
DETAIL OF
FACING CABINET

Instituto Allende

Museo Regional de Guadalajara

Disciplined treatment of door paneling, with the confinement to small areas of diverse rosette forms, indicates that this wardrobe was, no doubt, made during the third quarter of the 18th century.

Surprising to find on the inner panel of a door of an old church in secluded Pátzcuaro, this bit of carving, very likely inspired by the French of the time of Louis XV.

This version of a highboy with scrolled baroque pediment is, in silhouette, unmistakably Queen Anne. It breaks radically from tradition, however, in the use of lavishly carved doors to replace the customary tier of drawers.

Museo Nacional de Artes e Industrias Populares

A pleasing, small bureau, made in two sections, with an overall height of only forty-one inches. It is painted in Chinese red, dulled by age, with accents of gold. Floral designs are in soft, dark greens, in blues and yellows, with whitish doves encircling the Archangel Gabriel. Of particular merit are the restrained cabriole legs tied together with a drapery-like apron and ending in the customary claw-and-ball foot of Queen Anne models.

England, in the later years of the 18th century, made special furniture for export, many being finished in red lacquer to appeal to Latin tastes. Under this coating, cheaper woods were substituted for the favored walnut, often requiring extra framework to brace the legs. Local Mexican craftsmen copied both virtues and faults of the then popular "Queen Anne."

Villa Montaña

Two ample writing tables of pine. Contoured lines of legs with undulating aprons and omission of stretchers suggest another translation of Queen Anne features.

The Casa Alvarado, now a National Monument, was built in the middle of the 16th century by Pedro de Alvarado, a renowned officer in the forces of Cortés. This massive, fortress-like structure has been remodeled and is presently a charming home, filled with art treasures from many countries.

Among these is the four drawer set shown here and on the opposite page. It was probably made in Spain during the latter part of the 17th or the early part of the 18th century. Originally twice its present depth, it was cut down to reduce the projection from a wall. With shortened cabriole legs, the scrolled apron extends almost to the floor line. The hardware, bold in scale and crisp in outline, is particularly noteworthy. A handsome piece with a marked degree of high styling.

Home of Thomas Briscoe Miller

Home of Joaquín Cortina Garíbar

Small curved corner case in blues, holding white accessories. On a gray-blue background, lush swags, painted off-white, are caught up with dark blue and white cording, finished with white tassels.

Carved in relief, the softening effect of the pillow-like surfaces of the door panels with their rich scrolling give a feeling of voluptuous grace.

Home of Agustín Cullen

Chinese red, with geometric mouldings and ball feet picked out in gold, makes a lively contrast between cabinet and the curls and curves of the missal stand.

On wood head- and footboards, painted an olive green outlined in yellow, greenish-white doves and swags are intermixed with oleander-like flowers in gray-blues, shell and orange pinks. The swag, floating between two doves on the headboard, carries the following Spanish verse:

Dame tu mano paloma para subir a tu nido
Si anoche dormiste sola ora dormiras conmigo.

Villa Montaña

The lure of the mermaid is deeply embedded in the folk art of Mexico. Carved from rough pine boards, one was found, curiously, swimming across the headpiece of an old bed in a convent of Morelia.

From the far away village of San Bartolo Coyotepec, near Oaxaca, come these familiar marine subjects in black, handmade pottery.

A grapevine of rose-pink plaster with traces of blue, forms a pilaster of the entrance to an early 16th-century chapel.

Villa Montaña

Here a pair of jig-sawed wood door screens with fixed side panels and circular transom, become the impressive headboard for a bed. Detail at right.

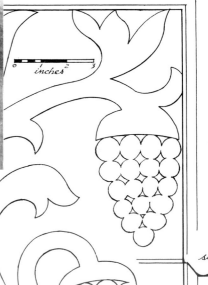

A grayed-mulberry wrought-iron headpiece against yellow walls, with
bed tables repeating the mulberry and the spread repeating the yellow.

Home of Robert F. Whitehouse

Home of Juan Hübbe López

The delicacy of the eyelet-embroidered bed cover with its dainty ruffles is in sharp contrast to the regimented balustrade of wood. Inspired by molded brick used as a screening, the design of the head piece is deeply rooted in the Mexican tradition.

(*Opposite page*) Catalonian painting inspired this *reredos*-type bed. Saint Martin surrounded by birds, flowers, animals and religious symbols in muted shades of blue, brown, purple, green, orange and gold, cut from textured cotton and appliquéd on a background of burgundy cotton with a chain stitch of black worsted, is depicted sharing his cloak with the beggar. This is fitted over a padded frame. The canopy of the same burgundy cotton, lined with gold, has a castellated edge, and is complemented by a matching spread covering two single beds.

The design and execution are original, created by Mrs. Whitehouse, a gifted artist.

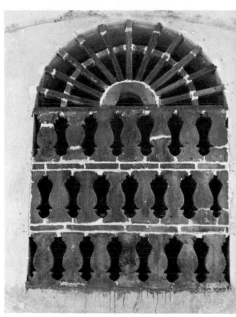

Hacienda Real del Puente

A modern headpiece with baroque and Moorish antecedents. Both backboard and the proud twisted columns are glazed a mellow off-white and tipped with gold leaf. On the eggshell bedcover, of heavy textured material, the coral sofa cushions recall the henna color of the carpets and floor tile.

Made in Guadalajara, this rare tester bed is an example of the wood turner's art. Two panels outlined with thin strips of bone are decorated with alternating inlays of pearl circles and bone daisies. Designs in gold thread enhance the underside of a rich red velvet canopy.

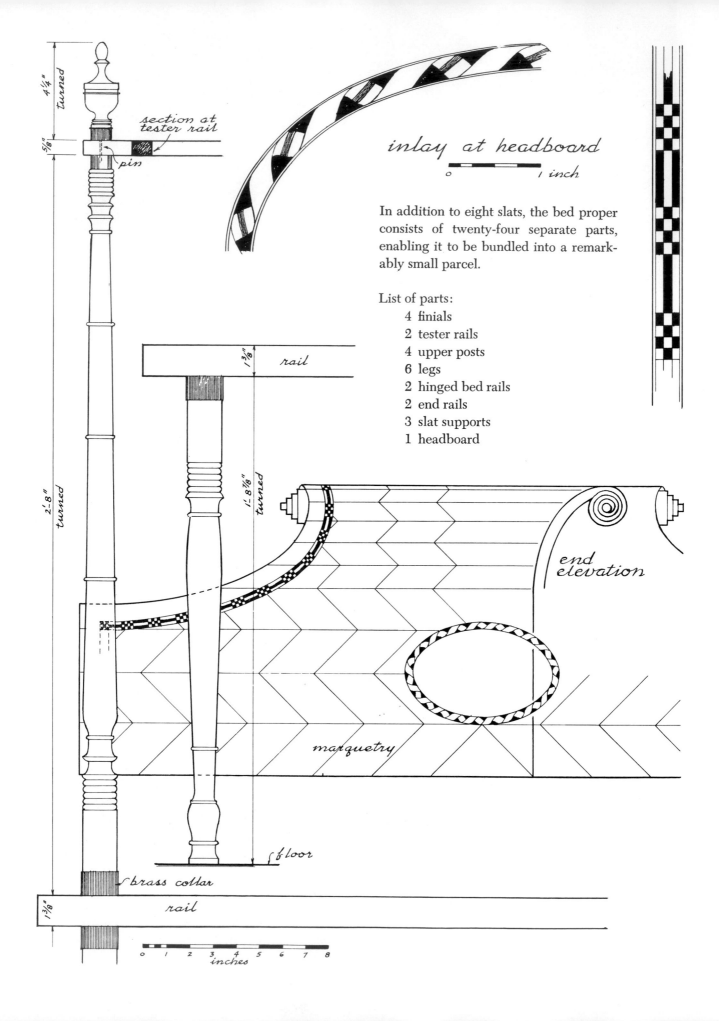

inlay at headboard

0 ———— 1 inch

In addition to eight slats, the bed proper consists of twenty-four separate parts, enabling it to be bundled into a remarkably small parcel.

List of parts:
- 4 finials
- 2 tester rails
- 4 upper posts
- 6 legs
- 2 hinged bed rails
- 2 end rails
- 3 slat supports
- 1 headboard

section at tester rail

pin

rail

end elevation

marquetry

floor

brass collar

rail

0 1 2 3 4 5 6 7 8
inches

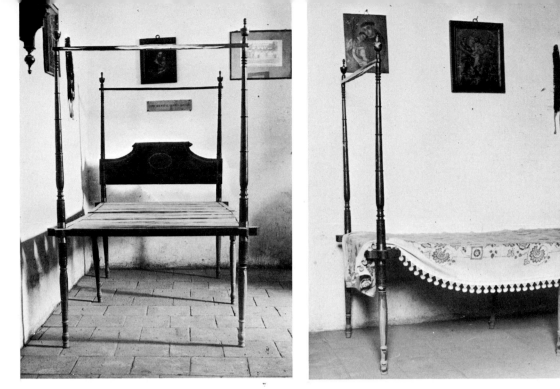

In the museum La Casa de Morelos, among many momentos of José María Morelos, are some formerly belonging to his fellow leaders.

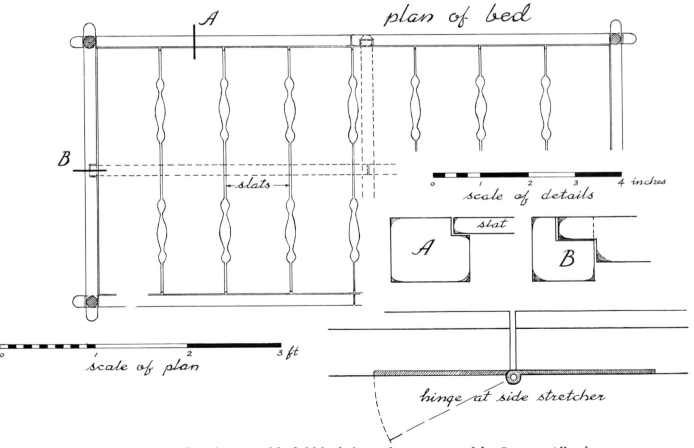

plan of bed

A

B

←slats→

scale of details

0   1   2   3   4 inches

slat

A   B

hinge at side stretcher

scale of plan

0   1   2   3 ft

The "catre," or demountable field bed shown here, was used by Ignacio Allende, who, prior to the Revolution, was an officer with the Queen's Regiment stationed in San Miguel. Not only is the ingenuity of this bed amazing but also its exquisite workmanship.

This strikingly elegant headboard of a matrimonial couch is embellished with a Spanish interpretation of Empire motifs in gold leaf. The wood of the background is covered with a thin coat of gesso painted to simulate a dark mahogany, except those areas between lions and around vase at top, which are a dull olive-blue. The relief of the decoration, low in relation to the cut-back field, has been seemingly increased by indenting its outlines.

Probably transplanted from France in the mid-1800's, this painted iron four-poster is a charmer. Elegance is the keynote with its medallions of flowers, brass fittings and the gilded ornamentation of the black posts, all crowned by the gracefully shaped canopy.

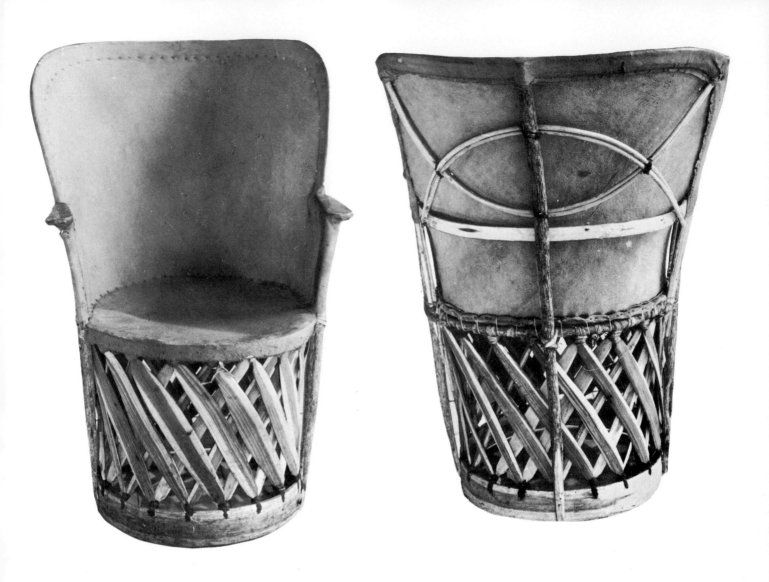

Some of the ancient manuscripts written and illustrated by men who followed Cortés in his conquest of Mexico, show the kind of chairs then used by the native personages of high rank. Known as *icpalli* by the Indians, this word was corrupted by the Spaniards to *equipal*, the name which has continued to be used through the centuries to the present day.

Originally, an *equipal* was one of three types but in general all had the same frame construction: a circular seat supported by a cylindrical base of diagonal cedar splits, terminating in a curved back formed by uprights of straight tree branches, reinforced by flexible reeds, with all connections lashed together by maguey fiber. The *equipales* varied only in the materials used to cover the framework. One method was to use woven rushes or *tule;* in the second the framework was covered with skins of animals on which the hair remained; in the third, tanned leather was substituted for the *tule* or untanned skins.

It is this latter type, made principally in the states of Jalisco and Michoacán, which is shown above. Known for their light weight, sturdy construction and comfort, modern *equipales* are widely used for porch and patio chairs.

The Huichols, an Indian tribe living in Nayarit and Jalisco, continue to practice many of their early rites. This oddly conceived and sturdy chair was used by their Shaman, the head priest of the tribe, in the performance of his ceremonial duties. The design of the back, with interlocking circles, is most unusual. The woven reed seat, edged by animal skin, and the criss-crossed bamboo splits of the base were thought to represent the flower of a century plant, the local source of brandy. When used during fiestas, this allusion was heightened by the addition of leaves from the plant itself.

Plan

Villa Montaña

The table with its top covered in pigskin, has the round base typical of the traditional *equipal*, while the chairs with their uncovered arms and backs are modern variations of the old style.

Plan

The chair to the left was a popular model during the latter part of the 18th and the early years of the 19th centuries. Its characteristic back is similar in construction to the Moorish type of screening so frequently used even today.

From Photographic Archives of Instituto Nacional de Antropologia e Historia

Another favored style of chair but of a later period. Made in the late 1800's, it shows the persistence of the baroque influence in Mexican furniture, both in the cutout of the back and in turn of the finials.

CHAIRS AND BENCHES   131

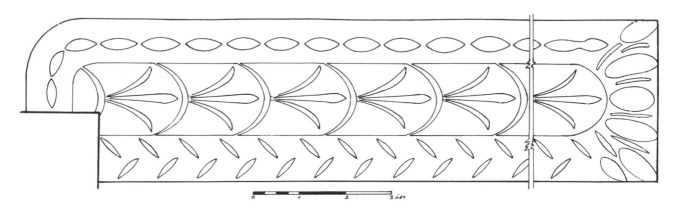

Museo Casa Chata

Odd among straight-lined chairs of the late 18th century is the overall orna-mentation of the broad, flat arms. The chiseled carving of this particular chair is shown in the detail drawing above.

nailhead

center

sect

From the Church of La Soledad, in the City of Mexico, came this chair, made in the early 19th century, and now in the Museo Historico de Churubusco.

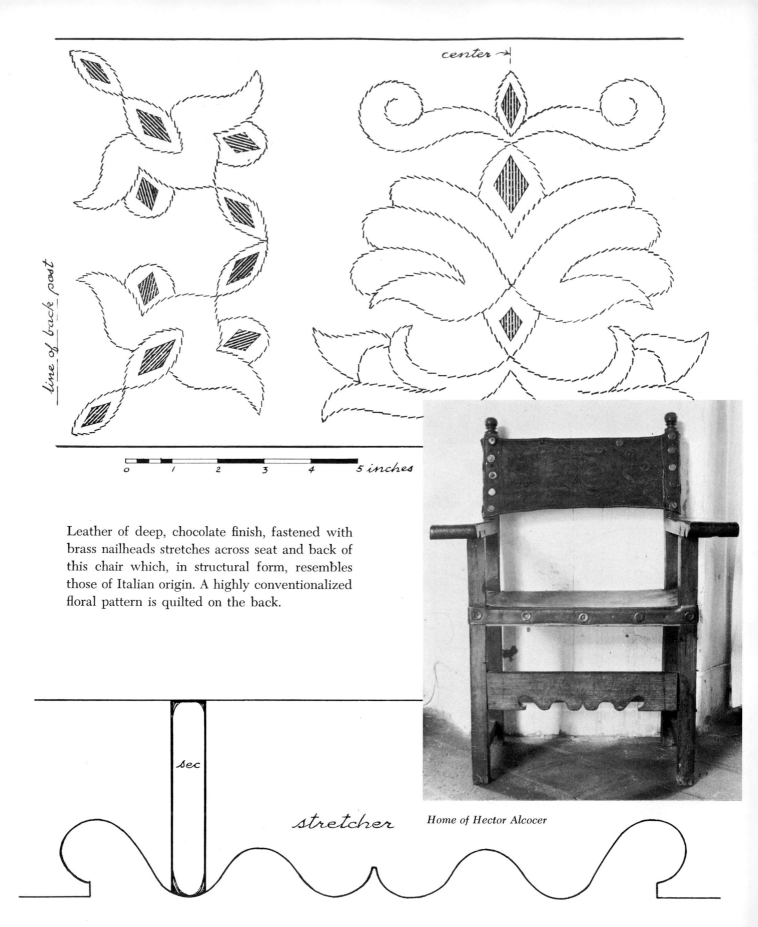

line of back post

center →

0   1   2   3   4   5 inches

Leather of deep, chocolate finish, fastened with brass nailheads stretches across seat and back of this chair which, in structural form, resembles those of Italian origin. A highly conventionalized floral pattern is quilted on the back.

sec

stretcher

Home of Hector Alcocer

From small, remote towns of 17th-century Spain came a method of surface enrichment made by grooving and gouging with chisels. Today, in the vicinity of Lake Pátzcuaro in Michoacán, this unique style of shallow carving continues to be highly regarded. The straight-armed chair pictured below, an example of the native craft of this area, has this characteristic carving spread over vertical members where, unfortunately, it has to compete, at times, with the coarse grain of the local pine.

Museo Regional de Guadalajara

Home of Alfred MacArthur

More impressive, with its deeper, cleaner cuttings and typical rosettes, both formal and informal, used as accents, is the shaped-arm version shown above, a true copy of a Spanish model. The leather covering of the seat was added later.

Museo Colonial del Carmen

Dignity and staunchness were bequeathed by the Italians of the Renaissance to the new Spanish colony through its mother country. Differing from other models are the broad stretcher, scrolled and pierced between the forelegs and the forceful sweep of the arms. Finials, similar to those shown, had been removed.

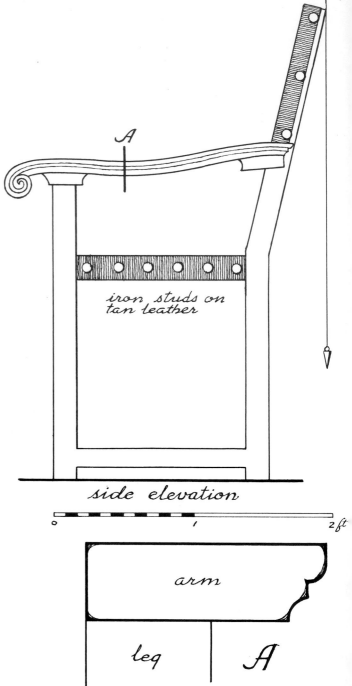

iron studs on tan leather

side elevation

0   1   2 ft

arm

leg   *A*

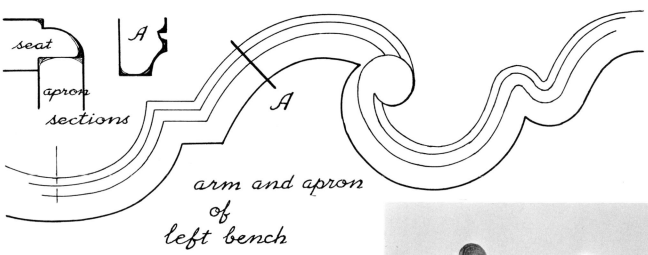

seat

apron

sections

arm and apron
of
left bench

A

A

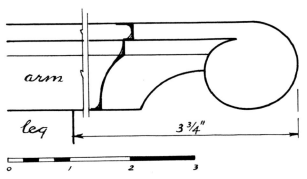

arm

leg

3¾"

0   1   2   3

Museo Regional de Guadalajara

Characteristic benches from the
end of the 18th century and
beginning of the 19th. The outline of their backs rise in the
manner of coattails, the arms
ending in incipient volutes.

Folk chairs in deep, dull red
with seats of woven henequen.

Painted in gay motifs of green,
pink, yellow, gray and blue.

Two benches, recently made, with similar baroque tendencies. That above, the product of a skilled craftsman, is beautifully finished, while the other, rugged and rough with its large nail heads, gives the impression of age.

Home of Humberto Arellano Garza

La Hacienda de San Gabriel

This simple bench was made at the end of the 17th century. Although scarcely long enough to accommodate two people, it is similar in style to much larger ones of the same period.

A low, diminutive bench with a fanlike back, quaintly carved. From weathering, little color remains except the black field with its center motif and traces of gilt in the triangular incisions.

Entrusted with the preservation and the dissemination of information concerning Mexican antiquities, the Instituto Nacional de Antropologia e Historia is carrying out its charge in a distinguished manner. Through the use of noted Colonial buildings as museums for display purposes and the publication of knowledgeable booklets covering a wide range of subjects, the Instituto is actively maintaining the great heritage of the Mexican people. Here, in the Museo Historico de Churubusco, a former convent, and described in a small volume *Evolución del Meuble en Mexico,* is this worthy example of late 16th- or early 17th-century woodwork. Made of ayacahuite, the massive bench was originally used in the Parroquia de San Juan Bautista of Coyoacán. The series of upper panels forming the back and their moldings are richly carved on the rear side only. Missing is the decorative panel formerly under the arm.

Two benches of pine in the Parroquia del Sagrado Corazón de Jesus in Queretero.

Both are unusual; that above with gracefully outlined openings stressing the length of its low back, the other with the vertical emphasized in a line of pierced splats rising from seat to top rail.

Replacing panels and moldings of preceding furniture trends, the Baroque applied superficial ornamentation as is shown by this cedar bench of the second third of the 18th century. Its incised scrolls and pierced motifs, further embellished with studs and lozenges of brass, are elegant both in design and workmanship.

Museo Historico de Churubusco

Happily blending the many characteristics of the Queen Anne style of furniture, the side chair pictured above was made in Mexico near the start of the 19th century. Comfort was commanded by the English queen. Ample proportions, undulating lines terminating in the cabriole leg, and a marked preference for the shell as ornament have been knowingly incorporated.

Few alien trends have captivated the imagination of New Spain and left their indelible mark until this day as has the Queen Anne vogue. Uninhibited, but without an excess of exuberance, is this playful example with its flaring *concha*.

Arturo Pani, Designer   *Photograph by Guillermo Zamora*

Photograph by Guillermo Zamora

A late 18th century "easy chair," which had somehow wandered from England to Puebla, was picked up there by Arturo Pani, noted decorator of Mexico City, to become his inspiration for this very elegant and sculptured version. The mahogany cabriole legs were attenuated, upper wings adroitly rolled back and the back given a zestful outline.

An endearing arrangement carved with chisels, combined with stiletto dots, decorates a diminutive table top slightly less than thirteen inches square. If this quaint fashioning were not sufficient evidence of its origin, the whimsical drawing of the woman together with her dress denotes a native of the neighborhood of Lake Pátzcuaro, probably from the village of Paracho.

In the magnificent monastery of Actopan, Hidalgo, it seemed fitting to find a lone cabinetmaker, aided by his very young son, carving and assembling an exact copy of an 18th-century table from another Augustinian abbey, San Augustín Acolman, in the Valley of Mexico. The reproduction shows the dominance of the Baroque in the furniture of those years.

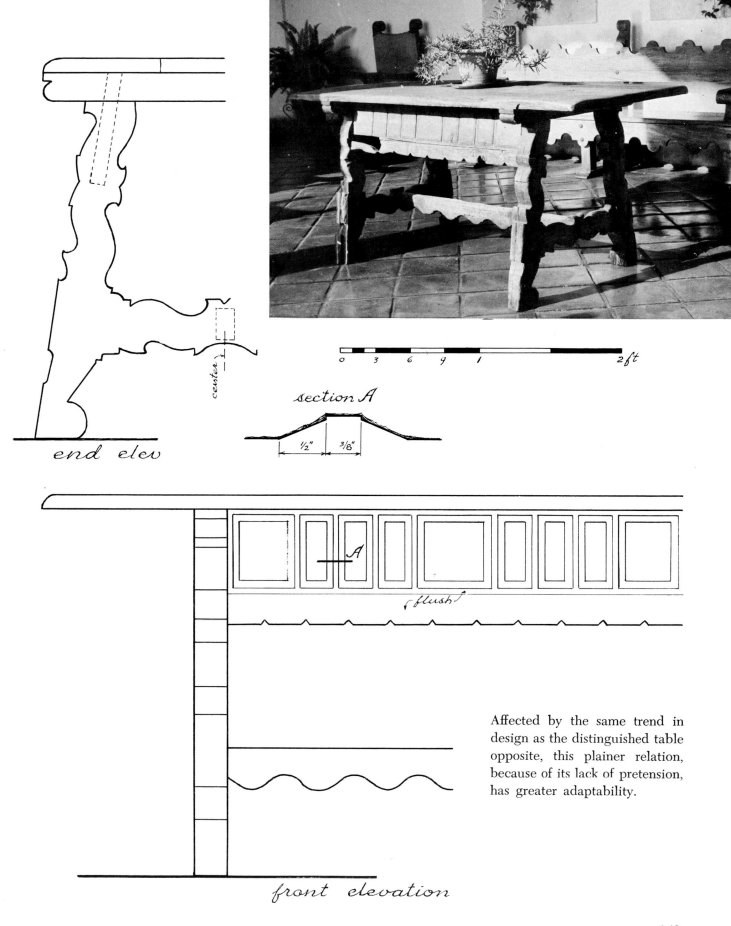

end elev

section A

½" ⅜"

center

0 3 6 9 1 2 ft

A

flush

front elevation

Affected by the same trend in design as the distinguished table opposite, this plainer relation, because of its lack of pretension, has greater adaptability.

Plan

Enjoying popularity for a very long period, that is, from the beginning of the 17th century to the middle of the 19th, a table with an understructure of turnings and a crisply carved apron above, continues in favor.

(*Right*) Originally gilded, an old tin wall lantern with embossed cresting and reflector.

The easy upward swings of the shaped iron braces, associated with tables of old Spain, are more rarely found in Mexico. By clinging to tradition, this small reproduction has an airiness due to the omission of apron and stretcher.

La Hacienda de San Gabriel

Casa Trini

Oddities may become very amusing in Mexican versions of foreign influences. This would-be butterfly table cannot fold its wings and drop its top leaves. All is rigidly fixed, then quaintly chintz-patterned.

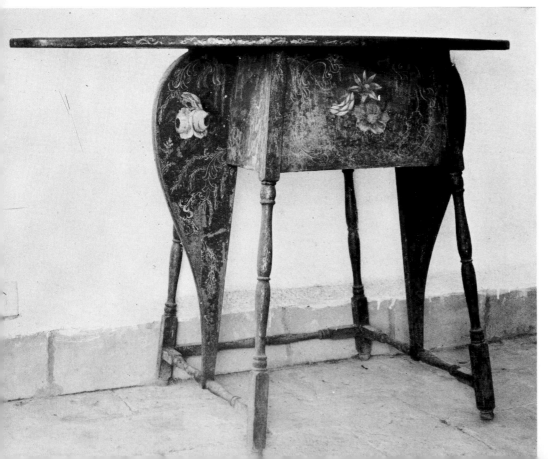

And, too, the intended drop-leaf kitchen table from the most southerly city of San Cristóbal las Casas, not only carries its single leaf vertically, but also the leaf is punctured by a drawer.

Forlorn and alone in the old Ex-Convento de los Once Patios in Pátzcuaro (now being slowly and thoughtfully restored) stands this perplexing console table. Its form is one of sophistication, but its legs of opposing S-curves, are crudely made and primitively held together.

Such delightful incongruities continually bob up, to one's puzzlement. We leave, wondering about these S-curves. Are they traceable to Europe or to the wormlike designs found on some pre-Conquest flat stamps?

CONTOUR OF TOP

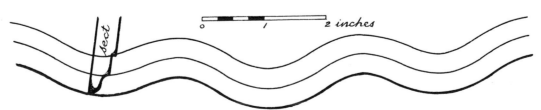

An ample top about thirty inches in radius, projects over a corner table of blond wood, indebted to the Queen Anne fashion for grace of line and plainness of surface. The ceramic urn above, a beautiful example of the style known as "Talavera of Puebla," has kept its tradition and European influence.

A droll story concerns this Chippendale-like corner table. Originally with a full circle top supported upon eight legs, it was fervently coveted by four admirers. By the terms of the will controlling its fate, it was quartered, and then a section was left to each of the four. This explains the unorthodox underbracing.

On exhibition at the Museo Nacional de Historia in Chapultepec Castle is this splendid console table with wavy skirting.

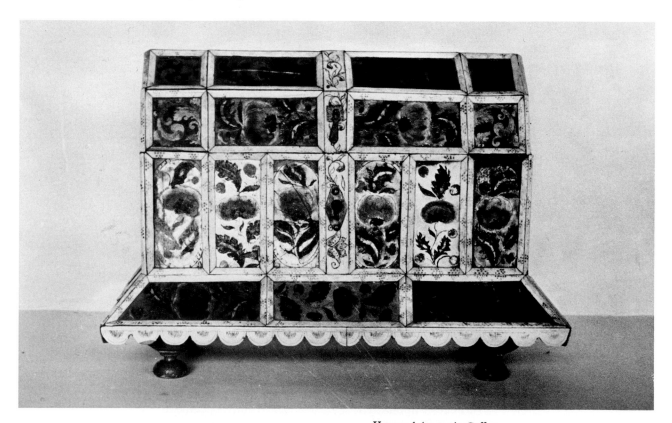

Of Philippine influence, a small box has painted glass panels held in place by the usual Mexican substitution of bone for Oriental ivory.

French cultural life, spurred by the power of Louis XIV, left a lasting impression upon decoration in Mexico. The curved line dominated. In copying, directly or indirectly through Spain, forms lost some of their initial refinement, but were frequently infused with a zestful and unrestrained exuberance.

Home of Joaquín Cortina Garíbar

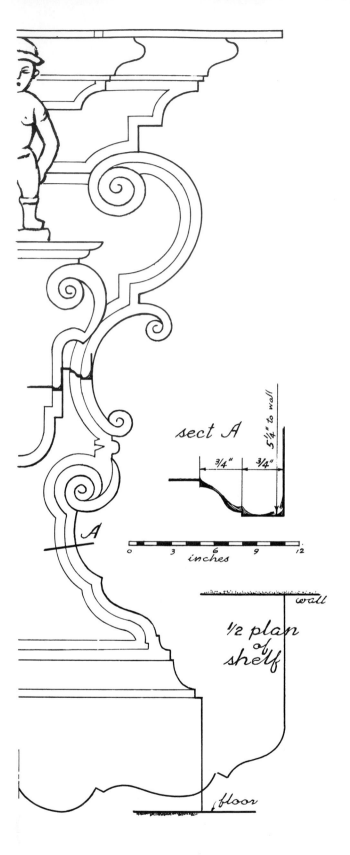

5¼" to wall

¾" ¾"

0 3 6 9 12

inches

wall

½ plan
of
shelf

floor

Painted white with edgings of gold, a
carved-wood pedestaled console rises
against a dado of Pompeian red in the
Museo Historico de Churubusco.

An exceptionally fine example of the old processional lantern, with its three-tiered crowning, symbolic of Papal authority. Originally carried on a pole during religious ceremonies with a massive wax candle to light the way, it now surmounts the starting newel of the main staircase in the home of Salvador Miranda.

Formed from tin having a high silver content, it has been preserved through the years with coatings of linseed oil until it is now quite black. The intricate and lacelike piercings of its upper bands (inherited from the Moors), topping a slender outline, convey a suggestion of stateliness and exaltation.

A lantern at a street corner in Jiquilpan, an old Colonial town in Jalisco. Possibly deficient in illumination but how fitting it appears nestling under shaped rafter tails and projecting roof bricks with their painted sawtooth design.

Home of Juan Hübbe López

One of a pair of bracketed lights on either side of the main entrance to a recently built home in Cuernavaca. Arcs of glass rise above a fragile cage, reducing the usual umbrella-like hood to an airy minimum.

Three rare wall fixtures, all with metal members of tin.

On the left, an open barrel-shaped cage protects a modern adaptation of the typical oil-lamp base: Instituto Allende. The old, triangular-shaped lantern below, with saw-toothed wings and cross-topped cresting, hangs on a stair wall of the Museo Historico de Churubusco.

Below, on the left, an exuberant blending of tin craftmanship and native design in the Museo Regional de Pátzcuaro. The semi-circular enclosure is formed with narrow strips of glass supported by the bottom shelf and held by delicately scalloped bands. The back-plate, richly ornamented with repoussé and incised designs, is unique. Here, the characteristic fish motif of Lake Pátzcuaro joins the medley of moon, bird, and a vase full of flowers.

Jardines de Cuernavaca

House of Giorgio Belloli

Home of Gordon Hicks

These hanging lanterns are closely allied to their architectural settings. Again of tin, elegantly fashioned, but supported by decorative brackets of iron. Of the latter, those enriched with lead rosettes had, no doubt, served previously as awning arms on city houses.

Designed by José Guadalupe Sánchez, this intricate, thirty-six-inch high tin lantern, hexagonal in form, is made up of 189 separate pieces of glass.

Home of Hugo Van Arx

La Hacienda de San Gabriel

Above, another old processional lantern. Octagonal in shape with finely pierced galleries and fluted hood, the whole capped by a regal crown.

Two wrought-iron chandeliers with interesting scroll work. Although found in widely separated places (the one above in the Museo Historico de Churubusco and that on the right in La Casa de Morelos) they are almost identical in design, with the latter an abbreviated version.

Home of Rodolfo Ayala

With the acquisition, during the 15th century, of many masterpieces painted by the great artists of the Low Countries and then the later occupation of the Netherlands by the Duke of Alba in 1567, certain works of Spanish craftsmen began to show a marked Flemish influence.

The brass chandelier above with gracefully curving arms and baluster stem reveals this heritage, while that on the right, with less of the Flemish and more of Mexico, is sturdy but with dainty flourishes.

Home of Jessica Van Beuren

The naiveté of the blossoms and free-standing leaves add a note of gaiety to this brass-framed lantern.

An elegant and ingenious design. Here, perforated brass bands in the base and hood alternate with lights of glass. Devised by Crisoforo Cruz and Son.

Hojalateria Llamas

Seen from below, a fanciful assembly of incised leaves and flower petals with the delicate tooling of the shaped base, combine to form a tin chandelier of refreshing design.

Photograph by Guillermo Zamora

Porcelain-like flowers in shades of pink were dismantled from a cemetery *immortelle,* found in Lagunilla, a flea-market of Mexico City, and merrily schemed around an old chandelier in the workshop of the distinguished decorator, Arturo Pani.

LIGHTING FIXTURES   169

Home of Agustín Cullen

Iridescent seashells form the flower petals of this enclosed fantasy. A broad lacelike leaf of coral lies on the raised floor to add, by reflection, its warmth of color.

More than the mere decorative note obtained by the use of rare saintlike figures as lamp standards, is the subtle quality of graciousness which emanates from them.

Home of Virginia Safford

Accesorios en Decoracion

Two solid brass lamps created by Pepe Mendoza, whose decorative accessories are, for the most part, based upon pre-Columbian motifs, modernized to conform not only to Mexican but also to international settings.

The rooster wears, over his painted coating of grayed-lavender, half-round stones of jade, turquoise, and amethyst.

Museo Nacional de Artes e Industrias Populares

Bona S.A.

Properly known as *palmerines*, these candle shields are at times called *arboles* because of their resemblance to trees. Fashioned of either tin or brass, they carry, hidden at the back, a short holder whose candle gives a flickering light. The resultant effect of throwing the lace-like pattern in silhouette is enchanting.

These are further examples of the versatility of the handicraft of José Guadalupe Sánchez.

172 LIGHTING FIXTURES

Hojalateria Llamas   *Home of Hugo Van Arx*

Tin candle holders of differing design. Both the rose and the pineapple are favored
Mexican motifs. Below, a unique and most pleasing mirror frame in brass.

Home of Donald Ryan

Scintillating with changing reflections of light upon angular pieces of mirrored glass, this stately edging gives an effect of vivid animation. Brass cames hold together the ingeniously fitted border members. Overall size, about twenty-nine by thirty-eight inches.

Bona S.A.

This distinctive tin mirror frame, about forty inches in diameter, is the work of José Guadalupe Sánchez. A ring of brass leaves surround the mirror, adding a color accent to the curls and flowers of an intricate design.

Carápan

An aristocrat among mirrors of tin, finely ornamented by repoussé. Made by the Xochitiotzin family of Puebla, who had been, like many others, artisans in metal for generations. Originally they worked in silver but during the Spanish rule, its use was forbidden except for special orders. Therefore, as most of their fellow artists, they turned to tin, following the same techniques and designs formerly used.

Typically Mexican in character is the ever-recurring sun motif. With an over-all width of about four feet, rays carved in wood then gold leafed, surround a convex mirror.

A cleverly contrived border of silvered glass facets, using copper cames as joining strips, frames this large rectangular mirror.

Taller Borda

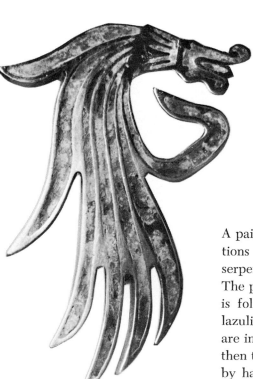

"Resplandor," above, a contemporary interpretation of an ancient sun god. Due to the smile it may be attributed to the Toltecs rather than the Aztecs, the latter being a sterner race.

A pair of door pulls or wall decorations remindful of the feathered serpent.

The primitive use of "Green Stone" is followed. Turquoise, jade, lapis lazuli and other greenish stones are inlaid upon solid brass castings, then tediously rubbed and polished by hand.

Carápan

Superimposed on lustrous silver, outlined and decorated in silver filigree as the ancient Mixtecas decorated their fabulous creations of gold, these modern works of art are given brilliance by inset pieces of turquoise, white and amethyst quartz, and luminous pearls.

Below, the Virgin of Guadalupe in all her majesty, with delicately carved face and hands of ivory.

Above, the Pattée cross forms the central motif of the Latin cross with its pendant angels.

Beyond comparison are the exquisite *Joyas Matl* or jewels of Matilde. Conceived and executed by an extraordinary Mexican silversmith, Matilde Eugenia Poulat, her techniques and designs continue to be carried out in all their originality and skill by her nephew.

The Virgin of Loretto with head of carved ivory and gown encrusted with coral
against a glorious radial background, sparkling with brilliants: *Joyas Matl.*

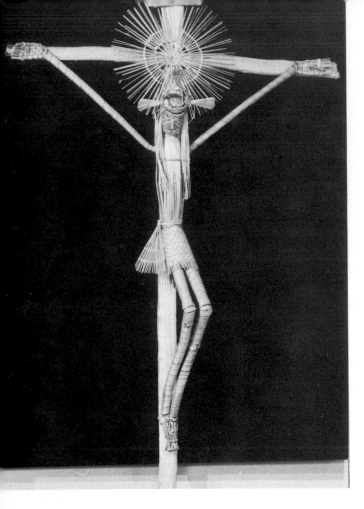

Deftly woven, wrapped and assembled from ripe stalks of wheat this crucifix was recently made in the neighborhood of Tzintzuntzan, Michoacán. As quaint and as ingenuous as its arts and crafts is the whirling sound of the name of this village. In Tarascan, Tzintzuntzan means "Place Where There are Humming Birds."

Museo Nacional de Artes e Industrias Populares

The memory of the founder of Pátzcuaro in 1540, Don Vasco de Quiroga, is "still fresh and sweet in the hearts of the natives of this region." Through sympathy and tact, he founded hospitals for the poor, wandering Indians, giving them care, occupation and religious instruction.

From a paste made of cornstalks, light in weight but dense and substantial, he showed them how to form the image of Christ above, which today hangs in the chapel of the intimate museum of regional arts in this town.

Employing the methods of 18th-century Franciscan craftsmen in remote northern Mexico, Mary and Child were fashioned in the manner of "folk art *bultos*." The head and hands are carved. The body is built over an armature covered with cloth that has been dipped in gesso and painted. This unusual statuette is the imaginative work of its artist-owner, Dorothy Whitehouse.

Home of Robert F. Whitehouse

CANDLES, GLASS and
HOUSEHOLD SILVER

The Mexican love for flowers is given added expression in these frilly, multicolored wax candles, some with highlights of gold or silver and all exquisitely crafted.

Sévigné Velas

"Avalos"

Twisted stem goblets touched with color. Svelte, tiered ornament mirrored in greenish silver.

Museo de la Ceramica

Three-unit blown-glass bottles, at times filled with colored waters. Below, a gracefully formed vase with brown-edged handles.

Los Castillo

"Avalos"

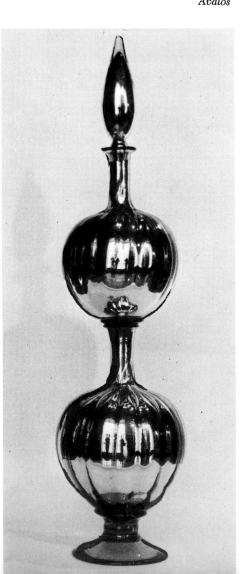

The ability to handle red-hot bits of glass while they fuse to form objects such as these requires a high order of craftsmanship. Passing a tree with gnarled branches in full blossom on which white doves are resting, are two carefree couples on their way to a fiesta in a flower-filled ox cart. The singing senorita in the rear is accompanied by her mustached caballero on his guitar, while those in front seem quite unconcerned about the progress of the bullock team. Truly, a work of incredible delicacy, as the cart is only three inches high.

In addition to the objects shown, which are, for the most part, only of decorative value, this same workshop produces hand-blown colored glassware, utilitarian as well as ornamental, in a great variety of charming shapes and designs.

"Avalos"

Taller Borda

Simplicity keynotes the work of Taxco's finest silver designers. Above, a large oval tray holds a teapot and some of its setting in the "Maja" pattern, gray-brown with flowers.

In high praise of the master silversmith of Mexico and his re-creation of a lost industry for Taxco, the Los Angeles Times wrote "Spratling brought more than freshness to his designs. He brought something recognized everywhere silver is prized, an understanding of the material . . . ."

William Spratling

William Spratling

William Spratling

188

Museo Nacional de Artes e Industrias Populares

In times past, these highly imaginative clay candleholders were used as ceremonial decorations on graves. The Archangel Gabriel stands at the base of this "Tree of Life," made in Izúcar de Matamoros, Puebla, surrounded by various farm animals, birds, flowers, and people, of subdued, rich coloring.

A very serious, small angel in blue kneels within a wreath of leaves topped by a radiant dahlia and three white cranes. This unglazed, triple candleholder from Acatlán, Puebla, stands twenty-four inches high.

The dahlia is veined in greens on a dead-white background, while the leaves of the wreath differ in color: blue-green, red, green, yellow, mauve, deep blue, then again, red.

Posada de la Presa

Another pottery candleholder from Acatlán in bright, yet soft colors. Here Eve gives Adam an apple while a red devil with a great, pink tail is gladly handing her another. This unusual tree is dressed up in black crosshatching, bearing red fruit and leaves of green and pink.

A ghastly Bishop, twenty inches in height, with missal in hand, officiates at the service for the dead on *El Dia de los Muertos.* His chalk-white skull under a mitre of blue-green is in sharp contrast with the startling magenta of his cape, over a cassock of purple.

Museo Nacional de Artes e Industrias Populares

In Metepec, a village south of Toluca, several families of artisans carry on the traditional craft of making by hand polychromed ceramics. Their work, happy, rich in form and coquettish in decoration, is very popular throughout Mexico.

Some are designed for amusement, as the seated rabbit on the opposite page devouring his carrots, while other pieces have a religious significance. This cathedral façade has to do with the Christmas season.

On either side of the entrance musicians play, boys swing and hammer the bells, the national flag waves on its staff and white doves circle the towers. Below, Wisemen kneel in adoration of the Nativity scene within the church. A truly joyful conception, and all done in reds, shocking pinks, yellows, magentas, greens, purples, black, silver and gold.

Museo Nacional de Artes e Industrias Populares

About half full-size, this native is homeward bound from market, her young son precariously held on her shoulder. Both mother and boy have the customary red faces. While she carries her basket and pitcher, he clutches a chicken with one hand and his hat with the other.

Unglazed pottery swans from Acatlán, Puebla. About seventeen inches high, with small predatory animals clinging to their white necks. The bodies are covered with band upon band of stylized motifs and pre-Conquest conceptions in varied colors: naive in design, yet ultra-sophisticated.

The captivating doves below were painted, as the spirit moved her, by a young girl assistant.

Carápan

On this and some following pages are examples of the skills, imagination, and artistry of the potters of Tonalá, Jalisco; an important town before the Conquest. Here, in an area rich in clay deposits, available specimens show that these descendants of the Toltecs, Aztecs, and Otomíes have carried on their production of ceramics during the past 350 years.

In a booklet entitled "Alfareria-Tonalá" by Isabel Marin de Paalen, the question of how this splendid pottery was developed is answered by an anonymous report of the 16th century: "He who teaches Man science, provided and gave the native Indians great ingenuity and ability to learn all the sciences, arts and crafts which have been taught them, because with all they have come out in such a short time, that crafts which in Castilla take many years to learn, here by only watching and seeing the making, they have become masters."

Today, these ceramic objects of superior beauty and quality continue to come from the homes and small workshops of various families who have specialized for generations in specific types of shapes, glazes, and decorations. Bowls, cooking pots, jugs, pitchers, plates and platters, vases, coffee and tea sets as well as decorative animals, piggy banks and diminutive toys comprise only a portion of the various items made.

The glazes have either a matt, or dull, polished surface, as these animals, or one that is hard and lustrous. Bands of fine black lines to form edgings, stylized animals, leaves, historical figures and emblems, and sometimes houses are the customary decorative elements. Basically, the colors used are similar: backgrounds, gray to beige with motifs in soft, deep tones of gray-blues and the gamut of siennas, applied with doghair brushes, held upright in the Oriental manner. With these forms, decorations, and colors, there is a continued mingling of the past and the present.

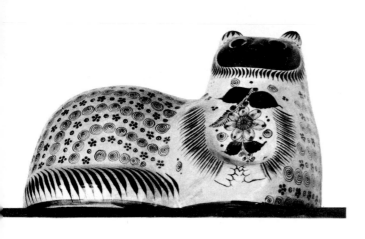

These modern platters, painted with great talent and fantasy, follow traditions of Tonalá.

Santiago, the patron saint of this village, is shown on the left in bright red cloak, astride a white horse. From the Museo de la Ceramica. The double-headed eagle, a Hapsburg motif introduced by the conquistadores, comes from the famed workshop of Jorge Wilmot.

Museo Regional de Guadalajara

This massive piece of earthenware was an early *tina de baño*, or bathtub. Animals and flowers are in bluish-blacks and earth reds on a pinkish-cream background.

Bona S.A.

The peacock and duck, above, are classed as *petatillo* pottery because of the fine diagonal lines which form a background for the floral decorations. In contrast with the hard, glossy surface of the *petatillo* figures, the others are finished in a dull sheen. Those, below, are known as *brunido de olor* due to the pleasing odor given off by the glazing materials used.

Artes Populares

Museo de la Ceramica

Some of the many shapes of a characteristic type of Tonalá pottery known as *bandera*, or flag, because it is decorated in the national colors. On a Pompeian-like red background leaves, flowers, and animals are painted in Spanish-white delicately outlined in green.

Talleres Tonalá

From Patamba, a mountain village in Michoacán, comes some of the most choice and unspoiled of native pottery such as the large plate above, and the jar and pitcher. The latter is glazed in dark green, while the others show their beautiful, red-earth clay. Designs are in white and green.

Below, two plates typical of Lake Pátzcuaro. Black, glazed, with motifs drawn in thin white lines.

1 *Museo Regional de Arte Popular*

2 *Casa Trini*

3 *Casa Trini*

4 *Bona S.A.*

Distinguished pottery pieces, highly glazed with raised ornamentation.

1. Covered jar, almost black from Santa Fe de la Laguna, Michoacán. Numbers 2 and 3 from Oaxaca. An old and honored swan pattern in thin, dark-green. 4. Black incense burner from Puebla.

"Puebla has always been a famous pottery center. Soon after the city was founded in 1532, the Spaniards taught the natives, who were descendants of the great Toltec potters, the technique of the Spanish Talavera. . . . . Throughout the Colonial period the industry was dominated by the Spaniards, who obliged the potters to make faithful copies in form and color of the Talavera de la Reina or the Talavera of the Queen — white glazed background with blue designs. As the native craftsmen are not good at copying, this pottery was inferior artistically. . . . . After Mexico won her independence from Spain in 1821, the Toltec spirit of the potters also rebelled. They began creating a more Mexican type of Talavera, with added colors and different designs. It was then that it became internationally known as the Talavera de Puebla. . . . . The best and most beautiful pieces are those made by talented potters who combine the Talavera technique with Mexican forms, colors, and motifs."

from *A Treasury of Mexican Folkways*
by Frances Toor

As this new conception flowered, many superb and representative pieces were selected by the great-grandmother of their present owner. On this and on the two following pages are shown examples of her rare collection.

A deep dish, fourteen inches in diameter, picturing a bowl filled with colorful fruit.

The Puebla artists of the mid 1800's and later were fond of depicting popular local scenes of the day. For instance, the platter on the preceding page shows a canoe loaded with vegetables being poled to market along the Santa Anita Canal from Xochimilco.

On the customary whitish background, the colors used were, for the most part, pumpkins, siennas, bright yellows, greens, blue-greens and earthy reds.

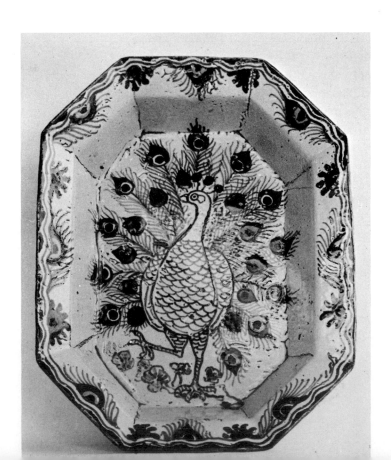

A strutting peacock completely fills the bottom of this large Talavera dish, found in the home of Dorothy Macdonald. Made over one hundred years ago, the design is carried out in blue with green eyes at the tips of the tail feathers and in accents of yellow and pink.

Gushing smoke, a small sugar mill lies at the bottom of a three-and-one-half-inch-deep jelly mold with fluted, richly patterned sides.

Within a simulated bamboo rim, a normally placid burro is about to throw his rider. This plate measures sixteen and one half inches in diameter.

A fruit vendor, his basket filled with bananas, mangoes, and papayas, sings his wares as he passes through the street.

The benevolent sun with flaming rays, a much favored Mexican motif, fills this fourteen-inch flat bowl.

Whistles for Mexican children and conversation pieces for everyone else. Some whistles from Oaxaca are quaintly traditional as the angel in this group. Others, like the mariachi player, are both past and present. But puzzling are the origins of clowns with conical hats and figurines in modish 18th century dress.

In *The Big Tree of Mexico,* John Skeating writes about the area around Oaxaca: "I attended a fiesta in the village one day when a dance was being performed in the square. The dancers were all men, some of whom were dressed as women. The costumes were copies of the 17th century Spanish court dress and, with the exception of one man, all wore white masks, gloves and stockings, and red wigs to disguise the fact that they were Indians. It was clear that the minuet they danced was taken directly from the Spanish conquistadores, although they had no idea of its origin and merely said that it was a traditional dance of Coyotepec."

Carápan

Casa Trini

Satin-smooth black pottery of important size from Oaxaca may be contrived into a variety of lamp bases.

Home of Dorothy Macdonald

On this and the facing page are examples of the unglazed pottery made in the small towns near Iguala, in the state of Guerrero. Mixing a fine white clay with shredded cotton, the Indian artisans seem to give a special color tone to their finished ware, similar to a very light *café-au-lait*. The decorations, consisting of ingenious bird, animal, and flower imaginations, and, sometimes historical events, are done in dark brown.

Although articles of many different designs are made, the classic water jars or *ollas* with their three-looped feet and two-strap handles are the most widely used. The decorations of the one on this page, made in the village of Tolimán over forty years ago, record the military exploits of a General Pacheco. They are reminiscent of those found on some Mycenaean pottery of the 13th century B.C.

Museo Nacional de Artes e Industrias Populares

PRE-CONQUEST STAMPS

from *Design Motifs of Ancient Mexico* by Jorge Enciso

DEER (MAZATL)

From Veracruz

FLAT STAMP OF DOG (ITZCUINTLI)

From Veracruz

FLAT STAMP OF SKUNK (IXQUILPATLI)

From Mexico City

In the informative introduction to the above book it is said that "it is a well known fact that stamps were in use in ancient Mediterranean cultures. Nevertheless, no evidence suggests importation from the Old World. Strategraphic research has shown that stamps in the New World have been in use since ancient times."

Originally hand-modeled from clay, and then baked in kilns, "the increasing demand led to the introduction of a new technique, the moldmade stamp for mass production." They were used by the Indians, who were well versed in vegetable and mineral dyes, to print skins and various fabrics and for the

(*continued on facing page*)

CYLINDRICAL STAMP SHOWING BRAIDED DESIGN WITH SHELL ORNAMENTATION

FLAT STAMP OF QUETZAL BIRD

Found in Chalco

FLAT STAMP OF PLUMED SERPENT

From Mexico City

ornamentation in relief of pottery objects while still pliable.

However, "after the conquest, their use was restricted to printing of trademarks, pottery, popular confectionary, and in some places identifications. Geometric design was common in the oldest stamps . . . Then followed naturalistic designs, plants, flowers, animals, and human figures . . . Naturalistic motifs became so simplified that they eventually appeared as conventional symbols, stepped frets, etc."

On this and the two following pages are a sparse sampling of the flat and cylindrical stamps illustrated in this stimulating book.

FLAT STAMP OF HERON MOTIF

From Veracruz

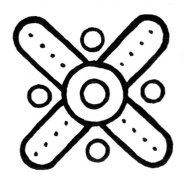

FLAT STAMP OF PATOLLI (A GAME)

From Veracruz

FLAT STAMP OF UNIDENTIFIED BIRD AS PATTERN

Found in Guerrero

211

FLAT STAMP OF MOVEMENT

From Mexico City

FLAT STAMP OF DOUBLE-HEADED BIRD

Found in Calixtlahuaca

FLAT STAMP OF MOVEMENT

From State of Mexico

FLAT STAMPS OF HUMAN HAND AS DECORATION

(left) From San Andres Tuxtla   *(right) from Texcoco*

CYLINDRICAL STAMP

From Veracruz

FLAT STAMP OF FISH

From Michoacán

FLAT STAMP OF DUCKS

From Chiapas

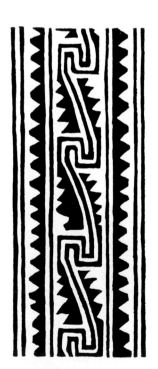

**CYLINDRICAL STAMP
STEPPED-FRET PATTERN**

From Mexico City

Casa Trini

A hand print in black-upon-white fiber paper by artist Walter Williams. Made from the rubbing of a stone found on the Yucatan Peninsula depicting a Mayan Plumed Warrior. Twenty-six inches wide, forty-four inches high.

Casa Trini

"Before the Conquest, the Mexicans used a variety of masks beautifully wrought of rich materials, chiefly for ritual and magical purposes. Priests wore masks with the facial characteristics of the deities during fiestas in their honor; and dancers, those representing the animals they wished to kill in the hunt. On occasion masks were placed on idols and effigies of the dead. For the latter they were of stone but for human beings they were of wood or mosaics, some with hair and golden crests. Many splendid masks have survived the Conquest . . . . .

"The use of masks, which has continued down to the present time, has greatly decreased with the degeneration of the primitive and religious dances. However, a great many are still being made and worn . . . . .

"Masks are made of wood, cloth, leather, clay, paste, tin, and paper, sometimes with genuine hair and teeth. They are painted, lacquered or left in a natural state. The features are subordinated to the materials and one finds in them the same plastic vigor as in the best and most primitive sculptures . . . . .

"If you were to ask a native why he wears a mask in a dance or at any other time, he would very likely reply, 'Es costumbre' — 'It is the custom.' Yet the present day natives are motivated in their use of masks by the same reasons as their ancestors — magic and the desire to achieve a facial expression for which they feel their own features inadequate."

from *A Treasury of Mexican Folkways*
by Frances Toor

The mask above is of carved wood, painted blue with red tipped horns, a gilded tooth, and a piece of mirror securing the shaggy, horsehair eyebrows. That opposite, from Puebla, is made of formed leather with symbolic painted decorations and crinkly black-wool eyebrows and mustache.

Museo Nacional de Artes e Industrias Populares

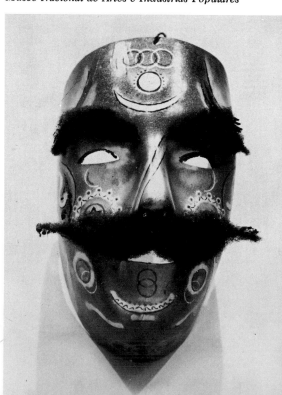

Below, an antique wood mask, painted black, with shaggy white goat-hair, from the state of Guerrero.

Above, wood "devil" mask, also from Guerrero.

Right, a handsome Michoacán mask enriched with inset pieces of mother-of-pearl, which not only accentuate the eyebrows, nose and teeth but also form a viper on its tongue.

Miscellaneous masks from several collections and only a few of the great variety which are, for the most part, still used in the regional dances of Mexico.

Tin masks are mainly used for decorative effects, when fine workmanship becomes secondary to the fantastic and grotesque. However, the gruesome caricature above, with five little glass-eyed goblins with protruding tongues, is unique in design.

The handsome fellow on the right was picked up in an antique shop in León. His lifelike face of wood wears a tin headpiece sprouting wispy leaves, flowers, and a reflecting mirror. An added novelty is a large saucer-shaped blossom with miniature electric light bulb, to flash on and off by means of a hidden battery.

THE DANCE OF THE CHINELOS

AT TEPOZTLÁN

For three days and nights before Ash Wednesday, the picturesque village of Tepoztlán, Morelos, reverberates to the constant sound of drums and bands. The native Aztecs are dancing their Dance of the Chinelos, "The Leaping Dancers."

It is a hopping, jumping, stomping dance with a heavy beat accompanied by a stylized rhythm. Originally, the natives used it to burlesque the pompous and often drunken antics of their Spanish conquerors during Mardi Gras. It has now become the feature of a colorful and unique fiesta, probably unmatched in Latin America.

The dance, which is the central feature of this exciting carnival, is more than a dance; it is a competition between groups of men from the individual *barrios* or sections of the village, to determine which *barrio* shall have the honor of representing Tepoztlán during the following year at other fiestas throughout Mexico. Due to the accompanying costs of a brass band, costumes, etc., only three or four of the seven *barrios* enter teams in any one year. The winning team is determined on three points: the number of dancers starting, their costumes, and the number of dancers on their feet at the end of this night-and-day marathon.

The climax is one of great excitement. The whole village dances, loud-speakers blare, horns and rattles are everywhere; what is left of the bands carry on, and several special dance orchestras make their contributions to the general medley — all this against a background of fireworks, and the explosions of aerial bombs. The general hilarity reaches such a pitch that the guests of the Posada del Tepozteco are advised to watch this final outburst of enthusiasm from the high terrace of the Posada rather than joining the melée in the plaza below.

Outstanding features of these annual fiestas are the fantastic headpieces and remarkable costumes worn by the dancers. Above, on the opposite page, is a headpiece which now hangs on the wall of the Posada, typical of those used in recent years. The mask of screen mesh is shaped to facial contours, painted in flesh tones, and embellished with a jutting black beard and heavy eyebrows, all of braided horsehair. (These beards, of course, are to caricature those worn by the Moors or Spaniards in bygone years.) The mask is then attached to an inverted *sombrero* which has been covered with either silk or satin and decorated with beadwork and artificial flowers in accordance with the fancies of the maker. And finally, to complete this amazing creation, it is topped with several strikingly colored ostrich plumes.

Costumes, worn in the early days, were made up of rags. Since then, they have evolved into flowing robes similar to those worn by the figure cut out from a travel poster. Long gowns of satin or plush in brilliant colors are held at the throat by a band of rabbit's fur. With the addition of a wide lace collar over the shoulders and a short, pillow-like cape on the back, the formal costume is achieved. The decoration of the cape, however, is another item which is left to the usually rich imagination of the creator. They are appliquéd with figures and enriched with pieces of mirrored glass, beads and embroidery. A recent dancer was attracted by the nudes of a calendar but his womenfolk obviously disapproved; the nudes were re-appliquéd with bits of lace for propriety. And so it goes in this peaceful but dramatic village of Tepoztlán.

Dance
of
the Chinelos
at
Tepoztlán

*Museo Nacional de Artes
e Industrias Populares*

An embroidered wool cloth from Toluca, with rhythmic border around a diapered field. Needlework of crewel, with amusing central motif, combines a happy array of colors: red, green, light-blue, brown, white, black and yellow.

Villa Montaña

Right, a *huipil* or straight, sleeveless blouse in hand-loomed cotton cloth, embroidered in red. From Huahutla de Jiménez, Oaxaca.

Above, portion of a large spread, sixty inches wide and eighty-eight inches long, in natural colored wool with stylized pattern in red. From Oaxaca.

Museo Nacional de Artes e Industrias Populares

From the Huichols

Plan

Peyote ceremonial hat from Nayarit.

Three shoulder bags of wool. The designs are woven in white upon background of black.

Arizona Originals

Villa Montaña

Small inwoven bag of black and beige. Overcasting of red, ends in perky tassels.

Below, sash ends from Toluca. Bordering in black with dark blue embroidery between.

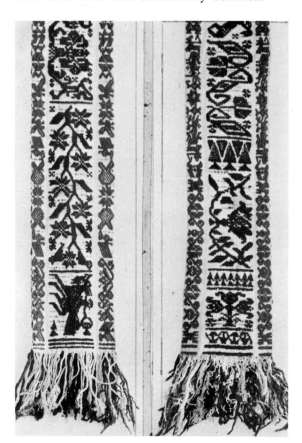

Right, portion of a black wool *reboso*, a long scarf worn as a shawl. Violent pinks, orange, reds, bright blues and greens are worked in coarse cross-stitch. From Hueyapan, Puebla.

Jeanne Valentine of San Miguel de Allende appliqués, over hand-loomed cotton, fancies in delectable colors with here and there an outlining of gold.

A native altar in the cottage of Pátzcuaro's winsome museum. Under a gay paper canopy of colored cutouts and against a panel of white china paper, slit and raised in repeating rosettes, hangs a religious painting, fancifully framed and double framed in tin.

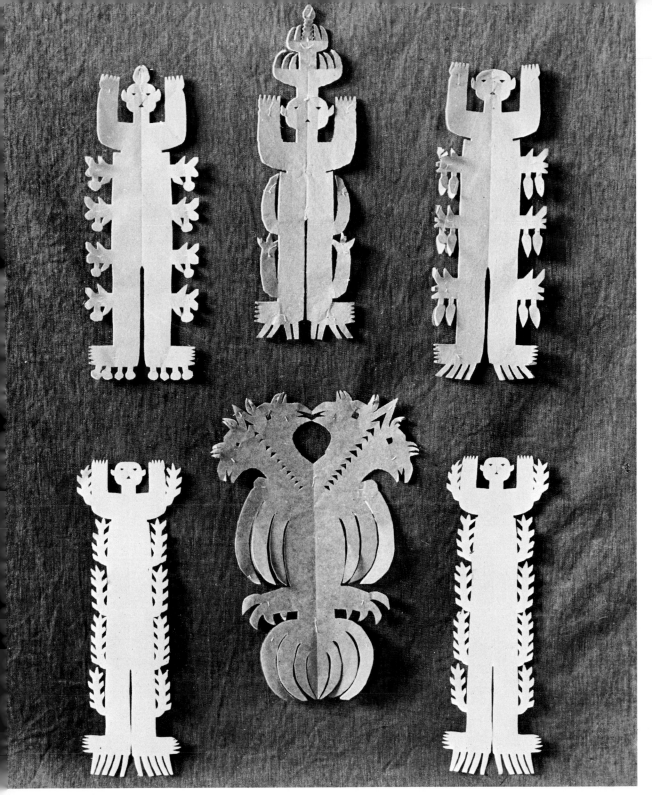

Museo Nacional de Artes e Industrias Populares

These delicate figures, cut from colored china paper, are known as *brujería* and represent spirits of Bad and Good. They are used by native Otomí witch doctors of the Puebla mountain country when invoking the health of an individual or the removal of an evil suffered by the community. In pre-Columbian times, the paper was made from the bark of a special kind of fig tree, called "amate."

Those of the upper tier are beneficial for crops. In the center, bananas, with potatoes on the left and red chilies on the right. Below, a four-headed eagle, "Lord of the Heavens," is between two cutouts each representing "Man of the Mountains."

225

Shop on Avenida Insurgentes Sur, Mexico, D. F.

A veritable Noah's Ark of frilly paper *piñatas* — *piñatas* gay enough to delight any eye, eagerly waiting their opportunity to add color and charm to a child's party. Burros, horses, rabbits, goats, and even a baby elephant modestly clothed despite her windblown skirt. Their appeal is difficult to resist.

White doves, small and large, some plain, others with glitter, are captivating touches to many decorative arrangements. With bodies of eggshells and heads of wax, the wings are fashioned from pleated paper.

A newly developed material gives a porcelain-like finish to the faces and arms of these colorful and most unusual "Gemma" originations. Some are purely conversation pieces while others, including lip-stick holders, bowls, and covered containers are useful as well as ornamental.

Below, Gemma holds a mirror to assure her friend on the proper placing of the beauty patch.

A recent addition to the rich marble cake of Mexican creations are the papier-mâché figures of Gemma Taccogna de Roth. The artist-sculptress is shown below beside one of her earlier works, a bust with a bizarre headdress, while to the right are her first-born. The objects on the facing page are typical of those being made now under her direction, employing plaster molds.

Photographs by Bob Schalkwijk

The paper lining of the mold, the cleaning and assembling of the halves when removed, the laying on of string filigree where required, and the basic paint coats are done by young Mexicans, some, outside their school hours. The colorful decorative features are then added by a small group of local artists. Later, the figures go back to the youthful craftsmen for antiquing and the finish glaze. The conclusion of this handiwork is one of ingenuity and delight.

Here are native Mexican papier-mâché figures with old traditions. The ones above are known as *alabrijas*, horrifying little monsters. Below, a small band of pseudo-skeletons with their bones outlined in black, wearing large, multi-colored sombreros, play and sing for the pleasure of the children on November 2 of each year, the Day of the Dead.

Casa Trini

During the years of the Inquisition in Spain, it was customary to burn at the stake on the Saturday before Easter Sunday, those who had been condemned as witches. This practice was discontinued with the outlawing of the courts whose business was to discover and punish heretics. In Andalusia, however, the day continued to be observed in the traditional manner with one important change. Instead of humans, the Andalusians burned these *alabrijas*, a combination of two words, *legartija*, meaning lizard, and *bruja*, meaning witch.

Brought over to the New World by Andalusians, this custom was enthusiastically adopted by the natives, who carried it on through the years.

Today, most of the *alabrijas* are made by a family in Mexico City. The unusual imagination displayed in their conceptions is extraordinary. Painted in brilliant, clashing colors, they are so purposefully shocking that they fascinate.

Carápan

Casa de los Tesoros

Prim and regimented are the *reja* crestings of Alamos, above and below.

Although wrought in iron, they recall lace edgings.

Home of William Walsh

The curve of this iron *reja* or window guard gives the impression of a bow window, with its airy grace, to an otherwise flat treatment.

Home of Albert Haywood, Jr.

Without the distraction of glazing, these wrought-iron transoms, foreign to colder climates, stress the silhouettes of their dainty members.

Home of William Walsh

Instituto Allende

El Convento de los Once Patios

La Hacienda de San Gabriel

A new wrought-iron grille protects this adaptation of a traditional quatrefoil window.

(*Above right*) Now and again, high on the walls of the patio corridor, are these octagonal windows surrounded by borders painted in earth-reds and light blues, outlined in black upon a peach background.

(*Right*) This circular opening with its carved-stone surround resembling the sun's rays, gave light and ventilation to a small bathing pool. It was formerly guarded by interlaced iron bars.

234 IRONWORK

rail

Home of William Burgess

sections

0 1 2 3 6 9 ins

0 1 inch. 2

new brass

old iron railing from Oaxaca

An old straightforward, wrought-iron railing. The handsome, forged newel post, enlivened with raised, elongated anthemions, terminates in a brass finial.

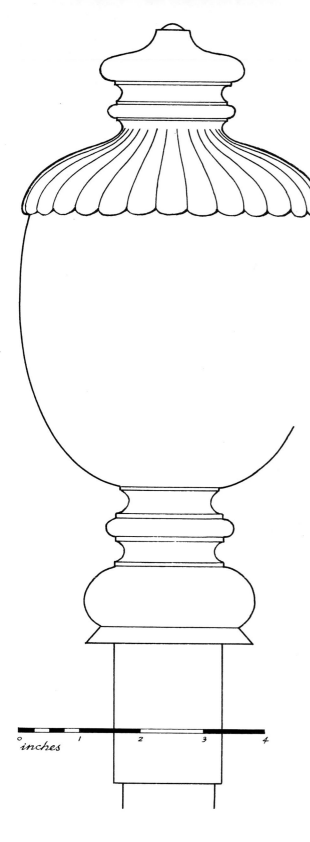

Guarded by an early railing from Oaxaca, a balcony overlooks the *sala*.

Home of Salvador Miranda

A stately newel with its linking balusters of iron was transplanted from Puebla into a portion of the historic Ex-Convento del Carmen, now a private home of rare distinction.

Recently installed in the 18th-century former home of the Conde de Rul, this old wrought-iron *cancela* with heart and lozenge shaped motifs is characteristic of its Oaxaca origin. It screens the *zaguan* from the patio.

Home of F. Cossio del Pomar

Home of Virgilio Galindo

Much younger in years and more intricate in design than that on the opposite page, these iron gates of fanciful tracery guard the rear of the *zaguan*.

(*Left*) Small geometric pattern of brick and pebbles, a paving suitable for extensive areas.

One of a pair of 18th century candle-stands. Unfortunately, the more recently added base detracts somewhat from the charm of this finely leafed scroll.

Home of Albert Haywood, Jr.

Casa Trini

A delicately membered peacock chair copied by a Navajoa craftsman from a magazine clipping furnished by the owner.

Recently made of wrought iron with cast-lead ornaments, these lacelike gates display the continuing skill of the Mexican smiths.

The terrace walls of a distinguished country home of the 18th century, on this and the opposite page, are brick red with raised work painted white. The edging motifs, the feather-crested masks on the piers and, finally, this Colonial gentleman facing his lady on the other side of the walk, make a conception unmatched in originality.

Museo Casa Chata

Below the projecting coping, terminating in three scrolls at each pier, is a tasseled, drapery-like scallop formed with mortar in high relief.

A carefully modeled container in the form of a grasshopper, a subject often used by early potters, with burnished, reddish-brown surface from Colima.

(*Below*) With vine-covered walls, a handsome double stairway leads to the main level of the garden which then climbs tier upon tier up the San Miguel de Allende hillside.

Posada de la Presa

Home of F. Cossio del Pomar

Villa Montaña

A carved stone monkey against a background of luxurious planting, guards the wide and easy brick steps to the main terrace.

The craftsmen of Queretero are now producing a pleasing variety of hollowed-out *cantera* stone garden ornaments like that on the left.

GARDEN ORNAMENTS AND PAVING 245

On this and the facing page, a narrow uphill site holds the peaceful charm of Old Mexico, vivid flowers and vines against white walls. Over the entrance, silhouetted against the sky, are the patriarchal cross and the three bells of the Trinity. In a recess of the garden wall, below, stands a figure carved in stone by the mason *maestro*. The owners wished a statue of San Francisco but had no model for guidance. The use of a picture of a boyish Saint Anthony, but substituting a dove for the beggar, resulted in this very youthful San Francisco.

Home of Francisco García Valencia

Home of Virginia Safford

The allure of the mythical mermaid persists to-day in the gardens and homes of Mexico.

Carápan

Home of Salvador Miranda

Home of Lorenza L. Story

Majestic is the rear wall of this patio. On roughly faced masonry of rose and lavender, a panel of chocolate *cantera* with twisted columns forms a background for a carved shell from which water, flowing from three small masks, spills over into the old, stone basin below. Softening the severity of the broad stone steps leading to the upper terrace are narrow planting beds, filled with violets, at the rear of each tread.

Two favorite motifs, a double-headed eagle and a pineapple carved in high relief, on this old stone candleholder.

Monterrey, an industrial city without tradition in folkcraft is now responding with ferver to the spirited ideas of one of its knowledgeable citizens, Humberto Arellano Garza, in contributing to the craft industry of Mexico. Garden sculpture, braziers, and pots of special design as shown here — a playful fish and dashing *conquistador* — are evidence of noteworthy and crisp innovations.

Carápan

Reddish, unglazed clay braziers and decorative figures show the whims of native potters. Obviously, the molders of the braziers took pleasure in burlesquing as in the vicious jaguar-like face on the right. When a slow burning fire tempers the cool of the night air, these braziers not only provide warming plates but beguiling, animated faces. The peasant, with an *olla* on her head, smaller bowls and basket in her hands and a baby in a *rebozo* on her back, is the work of Teodora Blanco who lives in a village near Oaxaca. In clay, she embroiders her figures with low-relief vines and flowers, showing a high degree of caprice.

Home of Ramon Martin de Compo

The ever recurring shell motif appears in the form of a carved stone basin at the side of a kidney shaped pool.

Home of Juan Hübbe López

Rising high above the reflecting surface of a pool, dramatically outlined against the sky, a pylon-like fantasy of fruits, carved with *cantera* of brownish cast, is of stately contrast to the calm, sea-green water.

Mosaics make a notable contribution to the stimulating variety of Mexico's building textures; their origin is buried in history.

Small pieces of colored stones, set in mortar with open joints, form a radiant sun and also an angel in the paving of this inner court. On a background of white, the designs are formed in bright tans, reds, and black.

Hacienda del Chorrillo

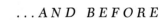

Home of Dr. Lucio Mayoral H.

A garage driveway of shaped concrete forming a serpentine pattern. Joints are emphasized by large, angular chips of translucent white marble.

AFTER FILLING OF JOINTS...   ...AND BEFORE

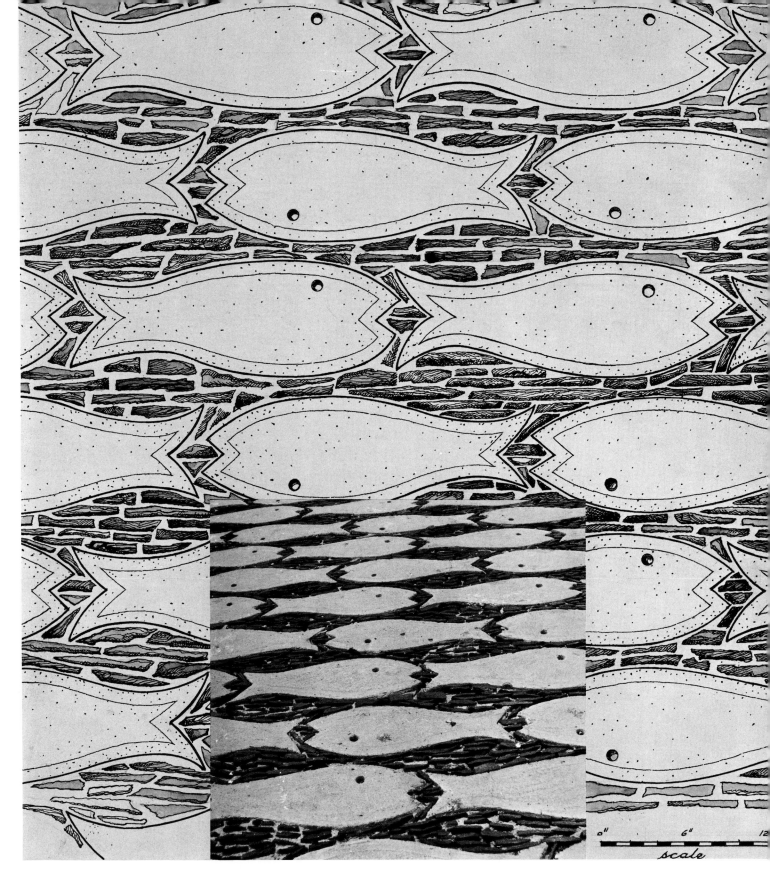

Fish, from ancient times a symbol of life, are a meaningful motif in the paving
of the Parroquia of Lomas de Cuernavaca, precast in white cement and set in a
sea of black stone chips.

Home of Rodolfo Ayala

Varied surfaces with their play of light and shade are inherent to this land of vivid sunshine.

Above, meandering through a wall of pitted, volcanic stone of muted grays and tans, are joints filled with slanting chips of pinkish brick.

Below, cantilevered stone slabs are embedded in a wall of the grayish-green stone native to Guanajuato.

Right, a plain column with carved, simplified Corinthian capital all from one piece of mesquite.

Home of Althea Revere